I0199743

Out of My Mind

Out of My Mind

Following the Trajectory of God's Regenerative Story

W. J. de Kock

With a Foreword by Tony Campolo

WIPF & STOCK · Eugene, Oregon

OUT OF MY MIND
Following the Trajectory of God's Regenerative Story

Wipf & Stock
An Imprint of Wipf and Stock Publishers
199 W. 8th Ave., Suite 3
Eugene, OR 97401

www.wipfandstock.com

ISBN 13: 978-1-49826-826-4

Manufactured in the U.S.A

To Marian, Carmen, and Zoé

Contents

Foreword

For many Christians, the faith struggles of W. J. de Kock will prove to be reflections of their own. While it is unlikely that the existential situations in which he found himself are anything like their own, it will not be difficult for them to understand someone's social construction of reality can be blasted apart by experiences that defy integration into their understanding of God's will on earth. Those experiences that deconstruct what were their respective "Christian" worldviews can leave them, as it did the author of this book, spiritually disoriented and socially in a state of anomie.

W. J. de Kock had been indoctrinated since his youth with a form of neo-Calvinistic theology that served as a legitimating ideology for a social system that defined his own ethnic group—the white Afrikaners—as a people of God, for a divinely appointed mission. That mission was to usurp land in South Africa and claim it as "holy" land which God had designated for them. W. J. de Kock and his people believed that, much as God had chosen Israel to be his people and given them a promised land that was already populated by the Canaanites and the Amalakites to be theirs, so God had elected the Afrikaners to occupy a special territory in South Africa and make there a holy nation to be governed by God's laws. Within their worldview, it seemed acceptable to treat the indigenous black people in South Africa as an inferior race, doomed as were the sons and daughters of Ham, and deserving nothing better than to be exploited as servants.

The God that W. J. de Kock saw as legitimating this worldview and its justifying ideology was a God who had ordained that "the elect Afrikaners" make themselves separate and pure. This necessitated and justified what, in time, became the social arrangement in South Africa known as apartheid. Living apart from indigenous black people and preventing any kind of mixing of white and black blood through intermarriage were social practices that had to be preserved at all costs.

To persons who have been socialized into such an unquestioned, closed way of thinking can come unexpected events that put cracks in their ideological comfort zones, and raise doubts that become difficult to handle. At first such doubts can be suppressed, but when additional doubts put more cracks in the worldview that had served as a protective dome over what had previously been an undisturbed system, there is a good chance that the once unquestioned worldview might tumble down. That is what happened to W. J. de Kock. Not only did certain events in his life cause such a shattering of the social order in which he had previously believed, but with that shattering came the demise of the theological construct that had legitimated it. What was particularly traumatic was that the God whom W. J. de Kock had been taught was the ordainer of that system became increasingly distant. It is no wonder that in the wake of such a crisis of faith de Kock fell into a "dark night of the soul." With the crushing not only of his long-held assumptions about God, but also his own identity, W. J. de Kock came to realize that his only hope for salvation was to be found in what he would call "regenerative theology." This would be his new way of doing theology.

Sociologists call this process "the creation of an alternative consciousness through praxis." Over and against the long-held dictum that it is what we think that determines what we do, sociologists, especially those out of the Frankfort School of Social Science of the 1930s, point out that there is a dialectic at work here. They say that it is just as true that what we *do* changes what we *think*. Reflection in the context of action is what they call "praxis."

In this book, W. J. de Kock tells us how events in his life, and the way in which he reflected on those events, forced him to dismantle the theology that had previously served as the ideology legitimating the oppression of indigenous blacks in South Africa and the creation of apartheid. In the process of reconstructing his beliefs—even his beliefs about the nature of God—de Kock realized he would be required to do theology in a new way. He calls this process his "regenerative story."

The reader will realize that de Kock is *still* in process and is continuously recreating his beliefs in the face of new events that require still more reflection. The author's new theology has created a new man, unafraid of doubt, because he now understands that there is more faith in honest doubt than there is in the unquestioned creeds of many who call themselves Christians.

Stanford Lyman, the one-time dean of The New School of Social Research in New York City, once said, "Life is absurd! And sociology is the study of how humans have tried to create meaning out of that absurdity." With this book and its author there is some similarity to what Stanford Lyman said that sociologists do. When his world became absurd, W. J. de Kock set to work, trying to create meaning out of that absurdity. He did this by employing what he calls "regenerative theology."

As he engages in this process of generating new perspectives on his theology of God and his worldview, de Kock does not do so as would the followers of Jean Paul Sartre. He does not try to create out of "nothingness." Instead, going back to the Bible and re-reading it under what he believes to be the guidance of the Holy Spirit, de Kock demonstrates for those who must go through the existential traumas that shake the foundations of faith, a model for handling such crises, which, as Soren Kierkegaard would say, "Leave any of us suspended in a hundred thousand fathoms of nothingness." W. J. de Kock offers hope for deliverance from such an abyss. He shares with all those who struggle for meaning, what has been going on in his own life, and the creative method through which he strives for resolution.

Tony Campolo
Emeritus Professor of Sociology
Eastern University
St. Davids, Pennsylvania
USA

Acknowledgments

Benjamin Franklin once said, "Most people return small favors, acknowledge medium ones and repay greater ones—with ingratitude." I will not follow that convention. While it is impossible to return favors, acknowledge, or repay all the help I have received as I wrote *Out of My Mind*, I would like to express my greatest gratitude to the people who have helped and supported me along the way.

This book has been in gestation for a long time and many voices, books, movies, conversations, images, sermons, and lectures have shaped *Out of My Mind*. It all started with a lecture by Archbishop Desmond Tutu at the University of Johannesburg (formerly Rand Afrikaanse Universiteit) in late 1970. It was the first time that I realized that there was something seriously wrong in my world as a South African. Many years later, on September 13, 1989, I participated with thousands of Capetonians in the last "illegal" anti-apartheid march. Mayor Gordon Oliver, Archbishop Tutu, Rev Frank Chikane, Moulana Faried Esack, and Alan Boesak led the march, but it was the presence of Desmond Tutu that had left the greatest mark on me. In his address, he reminded an agitated crowd that we had gathered as a "Rainbow People" to stand up against apartheid. And that, while we were seeking freedom we should act like people who can handle freedom—so he asked the crowd to disperse as people who were destined for freedom. I saw clenched jaws relax into smiles, fists opened into hugs, and rocks fell to the ground. Peace was possible. This march signalled the beginning of the transition to democracy. I wish to thank all those who shouted, whispered, cried, and danced until our minds became porous to the message of justice and until our hearts were filled with courage to act, to be different. Thank you Madiba, FW, thank you Desmond Tutu and the many unnamed heroes of the South African story.

Many students have shaped my mind over the years. More than twenty-eight years ago, I ventured into the classroom for the first time. I am grateful to all my students at Berea Theological College, Chaldo Bible Institute, Cornerstone Institute (formerly Cape Evangelical Bible Institute), University of Western Cape, Pentecostal Theological Seminary (formerly Church of God School of Theology), and Tabor College Victoria. More recently, I have had the privilege to lead and teach in the Openseminary in partnerships with University of Pretoria (South Africa), Tabor College Victoria (Australia), and Eastern University (USA). It was especially in these contexts that the ideas and concepts contained within this book crystalized in lectures and discussions. I am glad that this book finally lays to rest the question, "When are you going to write about this?" A special thank you goes to my students who inspired me to write, who exchanged interesting ideas, thoughts, and made this project a labor of love.

Over the years I have also had the privilege to minister in local churches under gifted leaders such as Jannie du Plessis, Lemmer du Plessis, Gert Horak, and Rigby Wallace. Each one of these men played a significant role in my ministry formation. But they also represent communities of faith that were seedbeds in which my faith could grow. I have had the privilege of being the senior pastor of three communities of faith. Bethany Fellowship during the anti-apartheid era was a place of restoration, Commonground (formerly Friends First Church) after the demise of apartheid marked a season of innovation that made space for the Openseminary. The small community that gathered under the name Commonground in Melbourne (Australia) was truly a communitas, a gathering of those who lived in liminality, as we tried to make sense of God in a post-Christian society. I wish to thank everyone who has shared life in various communities of faith over the years, your love, support, and affirmation has inspired me and has encouraged me to find my own faith.

I have also been the recipient of the gifts of many very gifted teachers. From my first experience as a student at University of Johannesburg with E. L. de Kock and Anton Pauw as my first teachers in Greek. Jannie Louw instilled in me a love for linguistics at University of Pretoria. Robert Crick confronted my racism and demanded spiritual integration while I was a seminarian—he remains a father in the faith to me. Other seminary professors like Harold Hunter, Steve Land, Christopher Thomas, French Arrington, and Rickie Moore restored my faith in the power of the Spirit and provided the safe place for me to grow connections between my head and my heart. Discovering the work of James Fowler, and benefitting from his personal input in my life, has been a lifelong gift—my signed copy of *Faith Development and Pastoral Care* is still within arm's reach from where I work every day. My doctoral supervisor, Murray Janson, was loved by many and he took my immature thoughts about faith development and set my foot on a lifelong path of discovery in the field of Practical Theology.

I want to thank my friends who appreciated me for my work and motivated me; those like Phil Glaser, Peter Russell, and Art Wouters who were early supporters of the Openseminary project and this book. Brian Macallan and I have been engaged in delivering theological education through the Openseminary for the last thirteen years. While we became coffee snobs in Cape Town and Melbourne, Brian and I discussed many of the ideas and concepts in this book. Other friends like Kevin Kriedemann, John Capper, Ian Weeks, and, most recently, Jill and Grant Exon read through one of the many drafts. Towards the end of the writing process I relied heavily on the well-honed editorial skills of Gordon Hunkin, whose insights enabled me to finalize the draft that was submitted to Wipf & Stock for publication. I would not have been able to complete this project without the help of so many willing and able readers.

I am very grateful for the early encouragement that I received from Brian McLaren, Chris Hall, Alan Hirsch, and Tony Campolo. I want to thank these authors for their encouragement. I will never forget Brian McLaren's kind words after he read one of the earliest drafts. He said in an email to me, "This is really a wonderful book that deserves a wide readership!" Your faith in my work inspired me.

While writing *Out of My Mind* I had the opportunity to present some of the material at a conference on Pentecostal ecclesiology at Bangor University's Centre for Pentecostal and Charismatic Studies. A chapter entitled, "The Church as a Redeemed, Un-Redeemed, and Redeeming Community," was subsequently published in Thomas, J. C. (ed.), *Toward a Pentecostal Ecclesiology: The Church and the Fivefold Gospel*, 47–68. Cleveland, TN: CPT Press, 2010. I draw heavily on that essay in this work and I would like to thank CPT Press for permission to make use of it in this publication.

Family is the most important thing in the world. My father and mother have been amazing parents. Being *out of my mind* could not have been easy for them, but their love for me has been unrelenting. They are my heroes in the faith.

When Marian married me, she married a politically conservative Afrikaner, but within two years her world was turned upside down. Living in a trailer park in Cleveland, Tennessee; the move to work in the arid soil of the informal settlements outside Cape Town; the political activism and the physical absences as I gave myself to ministry in an oppressed community was not what she signed up for. But Marian has been my greatest supporter, the most loyal partner and best friend. Her undivided support and care inspired me and encouraged me to find my own voice, to trust the process. With our two beautiful daughters, Carmen and Zoé, and the various dogs we have had over the years, she has turned houses into homes, meals into feasts, and pictures into works of art to make a space for me to be creative in this writing process. To these three very beautiful women in my life, I lovingly dedicate this book.

Ultimately, may this book be to God's glory alone.

W. J. de Kock
August 2013
Melbourne, Australia

Introduction to Join in a Theological Flight

In *The Matrix* Morpheus says to Neo: "You're here because you know something. What you know you can't explain, but you feel it. You've felt it your entire life, that there's something wrong with the world. You don't know what it is, but it's there, like a splinter in your mind, driving you mad. It is this feeling that has brought you to me. Do you know what I'm talking about?" It was a similar feeling that prompted me to write *Out of My Mind.*

I first became aware of the splinter in my Afrikaner mind in the late 1970s, when apartheid was arguably at its strongest in South Africa and Archbishop Desmond Tutu pricked my conscience as an undergraduate student. His lecture at our whites-only university was electrifying, annoying, and reality shaping all at the same time. When white supremacist students tried to shout him down, I found myself siding with the small number who wanted to defend him. On that day I knew there was a splinter in my mind. The painful process of integrating my head and my heart was initiated. When I try to remember the details of what Desmond Tutu said, I can't. What initiated the change of mind was not the words he spoke; it was not even what he did later in his political career; it was his way of being, his courage to stand up against the powers that dehumanized him.

Over the years that followed, it became more and more clear to me that my mind had been colonized by apartheid's theology—a pseudo religion. There were many unanswered questions, the easy answers provided by my childhood faith were just not sufficient anymore. This book tells the story of how important questions are in the process of finding one's own faith. Lloyd Alexander the American author of children books says, "We learn more by looking for the answer to a question and not finding it than we do from learning the answer itself." In *Out of My Mind* I have also taken

Albert Einstein's advice to heart. He is often quoted for saying, "If I had an hour to solve a problem and my life depended on the solution, I would spend 55 minutes determining the proper question to ask, for once I know the proper question, I could solve the problem in less than five minutes." David Dark says that we experience redemption, a change of mind, when are willing to hold "everything up to the light of good questions."[1] Just like Carravagio painted Thomas's finger in the side of Jesus, I need to find the right questions and then look for the answers. This would lead to a whole new mind.

On a trip to the United Kingdom, I used the London Underground. I was fascinated by the efficiency of the underground railway system, struck by how rushed everyone was, and very thankful for the safety reminders, especially the reminder to "mind the gap." The gap that is to be minded is the space between the platform and the train door. Because some platforms are curved and trains are generally straight, a dangerous gap could appear and if there is no device that covers the gap, passengers could fall or get injured. This nearly happened to me, but thanks to the pre-recorded warning, "mind the gap," I took evasive action.

"Minding the gap" is a great metaphor for this book. The gaps in my mind were at first small and even unnoticeable. But I knew they were there; I knew there were cracks in my reality. There was a splinter, or even splinters, in my mind. I thought I loved God; I thought that God was stern but essentially good. But now, the God of my childhood was somehow complicit in the crime of apartheid. I came to the painful realization that the many gaps in my thinking, emotions, and actions could be traced back to one big question—God? It was God after all, who made white Afrikaners superior to any other nation in Africa. It was the special relationship with God that made Afrikaners the new owners of the tip of Africa. It was God who made Afrikaners resourceful to fight their enemies, who were also God's enemies. This theology of apartheid shaped my mind, directed my thoughts and actions, and for many years it was how I made sense of the world.

But the inadequacy of this view of God was exposed by two very significant people in my life. Desmond Tutu's courage in the face of angry white supremacists at my university and a little black boy, the victim of his mother's addiction to alcohol. I was unable to show any pastoral care for this little black boy who suffered from fetal alcohol syndrome. For the first time, I realized that the land that gave birth to me was addicted to a far

1. Dark, *Questioning Everything*, 14.

more deadly drug and little babies were being born with a socio-religious form of infant fetal syndrome—called racism. But more to the point, the God that I worshipped as a child was seemingly happy with the hatred and disgust I harbored in my heart—I was baptized and filled with his Spirit after all. I was well on my way to becoming a white supremacist in a church and nation that was under his control. Was God the drug that caused socio-religious infant fetal syndrome? One has to be out one's mind to ask: "If God could allow his son to be tortured while he retreated to the safety of his throne room, could he then not be doing the same with all human suffering?" Or was it simply that the image of God being aloof and distant from the suffering of his own son had become my model for my own response to people who are different? No other questions really mattered, these questions needed to be answered—they were my sacred questions.

I needed a new hermeneutic that would enable me to understand difficult parts of scripture. How can I trust a Bible that seemingly justified the domination of one nation over another, that leads one to conclude the nations are in God's hands and that he can do as he pleases? How do I read a Bible that presents God, especially in the Old Testament, as an unpleasant, bloodthirsty, despot over nations? How can I love a God whose actions seem capricious, whose attitudes towards sin seem petty, and whose outbursts of anger remind me of the malevolent schoolyard bully who I often faced? While there is great improvement in the New Testament, one is seemingly still faced with support for slavery and male domination in the home and church. How do we read this book in the tension between the Old and the New Testaments? But perhaps even more to the point: How do we read the Bible in the light of the cross and in the liminal space as we wait for the arrival of a new heaven and a new earth?

But I also needed to find a way to do theology that makes space for the certainties and doubts I carry around with me. In *Out of My Mind*, I explore the role of theology in the liminal space between the so-called "already" and "not yet" of God's Kingdom. The theological method that is proposed in this text is in stark contrast to the system that supported apartheid in South Africa. In the text, a theological method is proposed that represents a journey away from theology that imprisons the person, and instead proposes a theological approach that is generative, generous, and productive. This approach to theology employs and generates generosity as believers pursue the knowledge of God through the integration of: (a) sacred questions that come from our contexts, (b) the generative tradition of the Story that we inhabit, (c) beliefs that transforms us as we follow Jesus through the liminality of the "already and the not yet," and (d) purposeful actions that create space for life as we attempt to discern the trajectory of God's regenerative action in the world.

Theology that is generative will embrace the uncertainties that arise out of the tension between our beliefs and behaviors, and re-mind those who practice it. God is a dynamic being who is on a mission in this world, and theology that has God as its subject could therefore not be static or a mere academic exercise. And if the world is constantly changing, and if God is doing a new thing in this changing world, then it is to be expected that God will also challenge our minds. Theology, by definition, can therefore not be static; it cannot be like a locked room or a bird in a cage; it must be more like a bird in flight.

1

My Mind

The Shaping of a Mind

Apart from the normal noises of our neighborhood, it was just another late 1970s weekend in suburban Johannesburg. My oldest brother was home from military duty on a weekend pass; my mother prepared a traditional Sunday roast to celebrate my brother's safe return. We had lamb, crispy potato wedges, rice, and my mother's famous caramelized pumpkin. We were just slipping into our blissful food coma when our quiet Sunday afternoon was suddenly interrupted. The screeching tires and the ominous sound of crushing metal snapped us out of our drowsiness and as one we stood wide-eyed on our front lawn. As the dust settled we noticed two cars were involved in a collision. One car driven by a big Afrikaner man had clearly forced the other off the road. Adrenaline pumping through our Sunday legs, we rushed over to the accident scene.

I have never forgotten what I saw there. The big burly Afrikaner man was physically assaulting the African driver of a badly damaged car. I knew the attacker; we had attended the same high school. After we graduated from high school I went to university and he joined the police as part of his national service. Although he was in plain clothes and in an unmarked car at the time, he had ordered the driver of a very sad looking Datsun to pull over. The driver did not comply. This gave him enough reason, he explained, to suspect that the driver was a Communist and needed to be stopped, even if it meant forcing him off the road. By the time we got to the crime scene he had smashed the window and was dragging and beating the badly injured body of his victim through the car window. My father and older brother restrained the policeman while I called the police for help. When they arrived, the Afrikaner was treated as the hero and the African was assaulted over and over again by the police officers. "You must learn to obey the white man, Kaffir[1]," was the last thing he heard as he was cuffed and bundled into the back of the mortuary truck, which for some reason served as the police vehicle that day.

I knew then that there was something wrong with my world, but at that stage I did not know the extent of it.

In 1976, some years before that afternoon when I was just fifteen years old, the Soweto Uprising exploded onto our newly acquired televisions sets. The Nationalist Government, with its apartheid[2] policies, infuriated the youth with its insistence that all scholars, irrespective of race, should receive their education in Afrikaans, the official language of the Government of South Africa.

Apartheid marked life in the South Africa of my childhood. I knew as an Afrikaner that the word apartheid meant "separateness" but my experience of that reality as a young white man was very different to that of other races. In 1948 the Nationalist Government of D. F. Malan won the whites-only election and they kept their election promise to introduce apartheid as a policy.

Building on years of colonial discrimination against the first nations of South Africa, the National Party adopted apartheid as a model for separate development of races. This model entrenched the perception of white superiority and the inferiority of black South Africans. People living in South Africa at that time where classified as European (white), Bantu (black), Colored (mixed race), or Asian (mostly Indian). Laws were introduced to restrict voting to Europeans only, separate living areas and schools were established, interracial marriage was banned and deemed immoral, internal travel passes for black South Africans were issued, and white control of the

1. The origin of the word is *Kafir* in Arabic and it literally means "one who conceals" or who is an "unbeliever." In the South African context it was used as a racial slur, similar to the word "nigger" in the United States of America.

2. Apartheid was a system that legalized a white racial oligarchy in South Africa. The United Nations General Assembly in 1973 defined the crime of apartheid as "inhuman acts committed for the purpose of establishing and maintaining domination by one racial group of persons over any other racial group of persons and systematically oppressing them." "International Convention on the Suppression and Punishment of the Crime of Apartheid," accessed February 10, 2012, http://untreaty.un.org/cod/avl/ha/cspca/cspca.html.

legal system was enshrined. I will return to these policies again later, but for now consider the words of Hendrik Verwoerd, one of the architects of apartheid, as he explains the basis of apartheid:

> There is no space for him [the "native"] in the European Community above certain forms of labor. For this reason it is of no avail for him to receive training which has its aim in the absorption of the European Community, where he cannot be absorbed. Until now he has been subjected to a school system which drew him away from his community and misled him by showing him the greener pastures of European Society where he is not allowed to graze.[3]

The new language requirement came as a big shock and it was just a bridge too far for the youth of Soweto. Their education was already compromised by a prejudiced political philosophy, lack of funding, and bureaucratic red tape. Even if their teachers were deeply committed, they were often ill-equipped to teach and always underpaid. In addition, dilapidated and inadequate school buildings, jam-packed classrooms, and a lack of textbooks dogged African education in places like Soweto. Under these conditions very few Africans finished high school, and now the added burden of Afrikaans would destroy any hope for a life beyond mines and kitchens.

On June 16, 1976, the frustration of more than twenty thousand young people in Soweto erupted. They ran into the streets of Soweto waving placards like: "To hell with Afrikaans" and, the red flag to an Afrikaner, "Viva Azania."[4] They insisted that if they needed to learn Afrikaans, Verwoerd should learn Zulu! Frustration turned into anger when the police opened fire on unarmed youths and soon anger burned as rage when pictures of the lifeless and limp bodies of those killed began to circulate.

The Shaping of My Mind

The Sunday afternoon incident exposed a crack in my own reality; a reality which, at that point was shaped by a theology that presented God as a sovereign being who determines the destinies of individuals and nations, the one who inspired Afrikaner leaders to design the apartheid system.

3. Quoted in Kallaway, *Education under Apartheid*, 92.

4. *Azania* is an ancient name for parts of Sub-Saharan Africa and the name preferred by those who were in the struggle against apartheid.

The roots of this view of God, this theology, can be traced back to the first settlers. In the mid-1700s the Europeans who settled in the Cape on the southern tip of Africa were ordinary Calvinist Christians. They were instructed to establish an outpost for the sailors of the Dutch East India Company. They are my ancestors. Most of these Christians would have been so-called five-point Calvinists who believed in total depravity, unconditional election, limited atonement, irresistible grace, and the perseverance of the saints.[5] According to Sheila Patterson, these earlier settlers based their existence in this new country strongly on the Old Testament, which was "like a mirror to their lives."[6] They saw themselves as a chosen people who were being guided by a sovereign, uncompromising but partisan deity whom had made a covenant with them, and not with others.

The story of Israel, the chosen people of God who were on a God-appointed mission in a heathen land, thus became the Afrikaner's story. Afrikaners were God's elect in Africa. It probably provided them with much needed comfort, as immigration is never easy. These settlers needed a story that would give them meaning and purpose in a foreign land. As this story entrenched itself deep within the souls of these settlers, the Afrikaner, or Boer, identity began to emerge. When the British governor introduced the notion of equality between black and white people in the early 1800s this Afrikaner identity asserted itself. The emerging theological understanding of my ancestors was that they were like Israel, God's elected people, and black people were the decedents of Ham, the cursed.[7] It would therefore be unthinkable that the "blacks" could be considered the Afrikaner's equal. The English may be able to live like that, but they could not.

The result was that thousands of Afrikaners left their homes in the Cape Colony—a colony that was then controlled by the British. In 1877, nearly forty years after the first settlers left the Cape of Good Hope, their migration, which became known as the Great Trek, had been reinterpreted as their latter-day Exodus. The Cape Colony became an Egypt to them

5. Total Depravity: Sin has affected every aspect of our humanity. Unconditional Election: God's election of individuals is not based on anything he sees in them. Limited Atonement: Christ died only for the elect. Irresistible Grace: the elect cannot resist the gospel message. Perseverance of the Saints: the elect cannot lose their salvation.

6. Patterson, *Last Trek*, 177.

7. See Sanders, "Hamitic Hypothesis," 521–22. "The Babylonian Talmud, a collection of oral traditions of the Jews, appeared in the sixth century AD; it states that the descendants of Ham are cursed by being black, and depicts Ham as a sinful man and his progeny as degenerates."

and the African wilderness was their path to the Promised Land. In this unfolding drama the British governor was Pharaoh and the Afrikaner commander, Piet Retief, was Moses. Later, after Piet Retief's death, Andries Pretorius would assume the mantle of Joshua. In broad strokes the Afrikaners used the Old Testament story of God's covenant with Israel to answer the questions of who they were, how they came to be, and how and with whom they would live.

As the chief narrator of the Afrikaner story, the church reinterpreted the historical events in South Africa through a Calvinistic lens. As a boy, I was spellbound by the lucidity of this covenantal interpretation of my Afrikaner history, and I gladly succumbed to its cosmogenic power. In my mind the stories of small groups of Boers surrounded by hordes of angry native Africans, of the power of prayer and of the miraculous interventions of God, all seemed to confirm the Afrikaner claim that we were God's chosen people in Africa.

There was perhaps no better example of this than the so-called Battle of Blood River in December 1838. This was the final and decisive battle against Dingaan, the king of the Zulu people of the Natal region. In the lead up to this battle, Piet Retief was led into a trap where he and some of his comrades were killed in Dingaan's royal village. Every time this story was told at school or at church, my arcane suspicions that black South Africans cannot be trusted would be confirmed again and again. It was clear to me then, as it was to those who told the story, that the battle at Blood River was God's way of avenging the murder of Piet Retief, but more than that, it was also God's opportunity to announce the arrival of his chosen people for Africa, the Afrikaners.

The battle lines were drawn. With Andries Pretorius as their new Joshua, 460 Boers prepared themselves for an impending attack from Dingaan and his warriors. More than thirty thousand Zulu warriors were reportedly on their way to wipe the Boers out—the Boers were once again outnumbered. Military strategies were considered, but this legend tells us that the Afrikaners also prepared themselves spiritually. For seven days they begged God in prayer to give them the victory.

Their strategy was two-pronged: they would build a *laager* (a mobile fort created by a barricade of encircled ox wagons) and they would make a new covenant with God—a covenant that would mark that day as a Sabbath for future generations to remember what God had done for them. On the morning of December 16, 1838, under the leadership of Andries Pretorius and Sarel Cilliers, the covenant was made with the God of Israel, the Afrikaner God. As a little boy, the outcome thrilled me: more than twelve thousand Zulu warriors were killed while there were no casualties among the Boers.

This version of our history made sense to me then; God was on the side of Afrikaners, just like Israel in the Old Testament. God empowered the Boers with supernatural strength and courage to win the first war of independence against the might of the British Empire. He also placed gold and diamonds in the mountains and rivers of their new land to secure their future. Even defeat could be explained—the defeat of the Boers in the Anglo-Boer war was to build strength in character. These stories filled me with pride as an Afrikaner and a Christian.

Some children grow up with nursery rhymes, but as Afrikaner children we had the added bonus of hearing theologically-inspired Afrikaner poetry. One of my earliest memories of poetry is a poem by a young Afrikaner theologian J. D. du Toit, who rose to prominence around 1908. He told the story of a young thorn tree growing beside the road. One day, a wagon wheel crushed the thorn tree. This was clearly a reference to the Anglo-Boer war, a war that scarred Afrikaners deeply. But the little tree was resilient, and soon it began to grow again. Even though the little tree was scarred forever, its scar became its mark of identity. As a young Afrikaner, this poem moved me as much as the crucifixion of Christ. I believed we must be willing to be scarred like that. As Afrikaners, God was also calling us to lay down our lives. Irving Hexham explains why I responded so deeply to this poem. "It [the poem] is a profound statement of national identity and political intent based upon a strong Calvinist's faith in God's providential leading of His people, the Afrikaner Nation."[8]

Another story that I learned at a very young age was the story of Rachel de Beer. In the winter months of 1843, Rachel's family was on their way to the "Promised Land," a land on the other side of the Vaal River (their River Jordan). The family noticed that one of their calves was missing. A search party, which included Rachel and her brother, was formed. Rachel and her brother were separated from the adults and became lost. The night was cold and the legend even suggests that there was snow about. Even as a twelve-year-old girl, Rachel realized that their chances of survival were slim, so she made a nest inside a hollowed-out anthill and covered her

8. Hexham, "Another Israel," 5.

brother with her clothes and body. Sadly, the brave, young Rachel died that night, but she saved her brother's life.

J. D. du Toit, the same Afrikaner poet who stirred many young Afrikaner hearts with his image of the Afrikaner tree, often evoked this maternal image of Rachel. In the Old Testament, the mother of Joseph was also a Rachel. So, Rachel de Beer became the mother of the new Israel—the mother of the Afrikaner people. Through sacrifice, the nation of Israel had been born. Now through sacrifice the new Israel would be born.

Through the sacrifice of Israel, salvation could come to the world. In the same way, Afrikaners were called to embrace their suffering in the name of their faith. Du Toit, as a skilled theologian and poet, pleaded with Afrikaners in the early 1960s (when South Africa became an independent republic) not to forget what God had done in their history. To forget would be to deny one's God-given identity, as portrayed in the idolatrous episodes in the history of Israel. He wrote this stinging reminder:

Woe to us if we forget God
as Israel did in Sinai
with wild idolatrous dancing.

It is now clear to me that the poetry of du Toit, and others like him, helped create the spiritual climate for the national movement that was gaining momentum as South Africa entered the twentieth century. All the time these narrators reflected an image of God who, while he was on my side as an Afrikaner, was easily angered and quick to judge those who did not keep the covenant they had made with him. More and more this view of God, and the mission we believed God had given us in this land, defined our Afrikaner sense of nationhood and the way that was expressed in the politics of the day.

When General James B. M. Hertzog formed a new party to represent the Afrikaner in January 1914, he was already a prominent figure in South Africa and a hero for his bravery in the Anglo-Boer war. He became the first voice for the Nationalist movement. The new political party was called the Nationalist Party—no surprises there.

Just before his untimely death in 1992, David Bosch, a famous South African theologian, pointed out that Abraham Kuyper's neo-Calvinism and romantic nationalism were two key forces at work in the birth of the Afrikaner Nationalist movement. Kuyper provided the movement's slogan—"In isolation lies our strength." In Holland, Kuyper used this slogan to rally and unite the small, scattered forces of conservative Calvinists and to spread their version of Christianity throughout the Dutch nation. In South Africa the motto was interpreted to mean racial isolation. Bosch says:

> For the first time in South African history, one now encountered sustained theological (or ideological) arguments according to which Afrikaners should neither fraternise with foreigners nor break down the walls of racial separation instituted by God. Like Israel, the Afrikaner's salvation lay in racial purity and separate schools and churches.[9]

The romantic nationalism came from Germany. In the 1930s there were young Afrikaner intellectuals, like H. F. Verwoerd, who studied in Germany. Verwoerd, who is often described as the architect of *separate development*, was Prime Minister when I was a little boy in the 1960s. I remember as if it was yesterday, how I marched in a brigade of young Afrikaner cadets. I remember how proud I was when I saluted this great leader of my people. I was only in primary school—Dr. H. F. Verwoerd Primary School—at the time.

Piet Meyer was another of those intellectuals. His version of a Kuyperian-Calvinist South Africa reveals how toxic theological stagnation can become. David Bosch gives us some insight into this view:

> His [Meyer's] definition of a Calvinist-Christian view of life . . . was clearly influenced by contemporary events in Germany. The organic national community is seen as a pyramidical structure with the leaders at the top who have acquired that position because of their charisma and drive. At the very top, we have the "natural leader of the people, called by God and endowed with the necessary authority to rule the people according to God's will." The leader called by God is apparently not elected by the people but only "confirmed" by them, since his authority is "organic." Political groupings who oppose the implementation of the national calling cannot be allowed to operate.[10]

This theological certainty led to draconian political policies. Ten years before the Nationalists came into power in 1948, the Nationalist Party declared its political agenda through D. F. Malan. These policies included restricting the right to vote in national elections to Europeans (the term used for white South Africans), and the reservation of the right for Europeans to work in certain occupations. Another declared policy was a complete

9. Bosch, "Afrikaner," 209.

10. Ibid., 210–11.

social segregation of racial groups. This meant that the movements of non-Europeans would be restricted, which would include the removal of non-Europeans from areas that were designated as space for Europeans to live. Along with geographically separate living areas there would be other segregation, like separate labor organizations and separate work areas. The Nationalist Party would also extend the Immorality Act of 1926 to all non-whites to prevent mixed marriages and to make it illegal for a white person to work for a non-white person.[11] All of this became a reality under the Nationalist Party after it came to power in 1948.

There Was a Time When Apartheid Made Sense

My experience of education in South Africa did not look anything like the students' in Soweto. The state was very keen to shape the minds of the next generation of Afrikaners. Through textbooks, lessons, and a retelling of South African history, selected cultural values were emphasized. Only the positive elements of our Afrikaners' history and the negative elements of our opponents in Africa received attention. Over time the differences between whites and non-whites in South Africa were deeply engraved in my mind. The views of Benjamin of Tudela, a twelfth-century merchant, summarized my views of black people at that time:

> There is a people . . . who, like animals, eat of the herbs that grow on the banks of the Nile and in their fields. They go about naked and have not the intelligence of ordinary men. They cohabit with their sisters and anyone they can find . . . they are taken as slaves and sold in Egypt and neighbouring countries. These sons of Ham are black slaves.[12]

In essence, at that time the differences for us were: white South Africans are superior while black South Africans are inferior; the Afrikaner has a special relationship with God and God has entrusted South Africa to the Afrikaner people; and Afrikaners are isolated like Israel, but God has made Afrikaners resourceful to fight their enemies and God's enemies in Africa. The Afrikaners' story, that we were God's elect who were given a new land, made sense to me for most of my childhood.

11. Copy of the Afrikaner manifesto is found in many documents. See Verkuyl, "Dutch Reformed Church," 204.

12. Quoted in Sanders, "Hamitic Hypothesis," 522.

The position of the Dutch Reformed Church, that the diversity of races was implicit in the command of God to multiply and fill the earth, seemed reasonable to me as an Afrikaner boy. God wanted human beings to fill the earth by diverging into different nations. I thought that keeping these nations separate was part of God's plan to populate the earth. What happened at the tower of Babel seemed to be a clear warning that God would not tolerate attempts to integrate nations. When people toyed with God's plan and refused to divide themselves up into separate nations, God became impatient with humanity and reasserted his original plan by causing the confusion at Babel.[13]

It made sense to me that we should protect our national character as an act of obedience to God and his purposes for creation. I often felt that the world was against us because they were against God. How could the world be so blind not to see that the apartheid doctrine and practice of separate and equal development for other nations was not biblical and a faithful response to God?

The apartheid theologians convinced me that God was doing something very special with the Afrikaner people. D. F. Malan once wrote these words and they settled deeply in my being as an Afrikaner boy.

> Our history is the greatest masterpiece of the centuries. We hold this nationhood as our due for it was given to us by the Architect of the universe. His aim was the formation of a new nation among nations of the world . . . Indeed, the history of the Afrikaner reveals a will and a determination which makes one feel that Afrikanerdom is not the work of men but of God.[14]

At that stage of my life, I firmly believed that we were persecuted as Afrikaners, just like Israel has been persecuted over the centuries. So, instead of recoiling from our mandate to protect the purity and sovereignty of each nation, and especially the Afrikaner nation, we should recommit ourselves to the Afrikaner calling.

As Christians, we are all looking for an understanding of God—a story that encapsulates our faith, that takes the Christian story and vision seriously, while also engaging the questions and experiences of everyday life. For twenty-two years apartheid seemed reasonable to me, and it functioned as a centripetal force that ordered and gave meaning my life. It supported

13. See Bax, "Bible and Apartheid," 114–18.

14. Pienaar, *Glo in U Volk*, 235–36. The title can be translated as "Believe in Your Nation."

and sustained our lives as newcomers on the Southern tip of Africa, it gave orientation, courage, meaning, and hope to our lives. Apartheid, as a theology of story, was able to unite us into a community of shared interpretation, loyalty, and trust.

And Then It Didn't Make Sense Anymore

At university I began to read more widely about politics, even if at first it was done for self-preservation. I was surprised at what I could find, even with all the censorship that was around. When the European settlers came to the southern tip of Africa in 1652 they also quickly overpowered the first inhabitants of Southern Africa. One of Desmond Tutu's humorous quotes offers this insight: "When the missionaries came to Africa they had the Bible and we had the land. They said 'Let us pray.' We closed our eyes. When we opened them we had the Bible and they had the land."

Slaves were brought from other parts of the world and from Africa to assist the settlers in establishing farms. Since none of the slaves were European, they could not be white, so they too were first classified as non-European.[15] Racial classification was the colonial way South Africa tried to answer the troubling questions of race and race relations. Despite this, the history of the Cape Colony reveals that many intimate relationships were formed across the racial lines of division and that many children were born who defied the imposed labeling. Some authors even suggested that being "white" in South Africa is a myth.[16] I learned that, before the British colonized the Cape Colony in 1795, all children born from relationships between white men and slaves were regarded and accepted as being white.

As we noted before, under apartheid, the 1948 Nationalist Government, which claimed that it wanted to promote separate but equal development, introduced the new racial labeling system. The most surprising category was this one: those who were a blend of black and white were not called grey, as you would expect, they were called "colored." Their skin color was neither black nor white; it was more like the color of the sand of the beautiful beaches of the Cape of Good Hope.

15. This was the historic basis for the apartheid policies that were developed in the twentieth century.

16. See the research done in 1971 by J. A. Heese, and the startling revelations of H. F. Heese in 1984. The work of H. F. Heese sparked heated debate and even fist fights in parliament in 1985. See Michael Parks's article, "Racial Purists," LA Times, March 5, 1985.

When the first settlers encountered the nomadic Khoisan people who roamed the beaches of the Western Cape, they at first thought of them as "black," but now this new classification would take care of them too. Not everything was a simple as that though. What of those children born as a result of a European master having sexual intercourse with his non-European servant? Would these children be colored in exactly the same way as the offspring of two Malaysian slaves? Much to the chagrin of the policy-makers of apartheid, the system of racial classification did not answer all the questions about race relationships. John Nauright, many years later, explains it like this:

> The issue of Colored South Africans was a particularly difficult one for the government and for whites. Many whites had some African or Colored blood in their distant past, though they did not want to admit to any such traces, as this went against the construction of racial separateness. Additionally, many Coloreds had come to South Africa initially as slaves and were linked to the menial tasks that Africans performed in areas outside the Western Cape. The majority of Coloreds spoke Afrikaans, and along with the blood relations, this made definitions of the Volk and of Afrikanerdom difficult.[17]

While apartheid had separate but equal development as its main doctrine, it did not work this way in practice, and I became increasingly aware of it. In the early 1980s white South Africans made up 18 percent of the total population and received 72 percent of the national income. White South Africans claimed 87 percent of the land, while the remaining 13 percent was "given" to the other race groups.

Desmond Tutu's assessment of the incongruence between the stated objectives and practical consequences of apartheid was my first insight into the misery that apartheid was causing. His words unsettled me and my naïve childhood faith found it difficult to cope. He wrote,

> The policy demands the uprooting of millions (at the last count over two million) of Blacks from their homes to be dumped in arid, often inaccessible, so-called resettlement camps in bantustans, those ghettos of poverty and misery, inexhaustible reservoirs of cheap labor. I have visited many such dumping grounds and will never forget the little girl who said that when there is no food to borrow, they drink water to fill their stomachs. People starve in a

17. Nauright, *Sport, Cultures, and Identities*, 95.

> land of record crop surpluses, because of a deliberate government policy.[18]

I could see that apartheid was built on the premise that the value of a person can be determined by the color of her or his skin and that human ideas and passions can be controlled by fear. While apartheid managed, through martial law and other forms of intimidation, to control the day-to-day behaviors of people in South Africa for decades, I wondered if it could quash human thoughts and passions. I knew that Mahatma Ghandi, who also experienced racism in South Africa when it was still a British colony, once said, "You can chain me, you can torture me, you can even destroy this body, but you will never imprison my mind." I began to wonder if apartheid could stop the human quest for freedom.

Out of My Mind

This was the Afrikaner world that shaped my mind. But *unscripted events*, like the unsettling Sunday afternoon scene and the pictures of police in armed vehicles chasing small children in Soweto, cracked the veneer of my privileged Afrikaner reality. Could it be that we were living in a reality created by mad men in pinstriped suits and top hats? Could it be that my world was an unsustainable reality built on illusions and fantasy? Could it be that God was in fact not directing society in favor of the Afrikaner, as I had been told? Or, is there even a God?

I asked these questions as a young Christian man living in an apartheid South Africa. Today, thirty years later, I look back and I can see how my mind has changed—but most of all how my view of God has been transformed.

I am reminded what Karl Barth once said, that doing theology is like painting a bird in flight, and that we do theology as pilgrims—*theologia viatorum*. As such, our theology can never be complete, or never be beyond the need for improvement. In retrospect, my experience of theology in South Africa was in stark contrast to Karl Barth's hopeful expectation. I would say that metaphors of stagnation would be more appropriate to describe the brand of theology that nurtured my young Afrikaner soul. The theology that undergirded apartheid in South Africa, as elsewhere in the world, was constrained and constraining. I was aware of how I felt locked

18. Bax, *Apartheid*, 46.

up, but I did not yet know that my view of God was the cause. But the Sunday afternoon scene and the Soweto Uprising opened the cage of my mind, even if initially it was just barely open.

In the pages that follow I will attempt to paint a picture of the trajectory that my faith in God has taken over the last thirty years. What follows is my attempt to tell the story of that theological flight. It tells the story of how I had to get *out of my mind*, but it also acknowledges that these thoughts are *out of my mind*.

2

Splintered Mind

A Quest for Faith to Live By

As I write about the emergence of cracks in my Afrikaner reality and the theology that supported it, I am reminded of two movies from the late 1990s. In Peter Weir's film *The Truman Show* (1998) Christof, the director of a reality show, has complete control over Truman's life. Truman is the main character in the reality show but he does not know it is only a show. The whole world can tune in to watch Truman's life unfold in real time. Although Truman has no idea that his life is scripted and unfolding on a Hollywood movie set, everyone else knows the truth and is playing along. One of Christof's greatest fears is that one of the actors will slip up or act out of character and make Truman suspicious; that he will realize that this is all just a social experiment and his life has been a fake existence.

The director's fear progressively becomes a reality with a series of unscripted events. A stage light (invisible from the ground) falls from the sky, Truman's wife, Sylvia, cannot respond to his declaration of love and she lets it slip that this is all just a show. When Truman acts in a threatening manner towards her later in the film, she calls on Christof to "do something." In a dramatic scene, Truman decides to escape and launches a boat into the sea. After a near-death experience he eventually runs into the end of the stage set. At this point he not only finally knows that his life is a fake, but for the first time in his life he is able to make his own decisions. He decides to leave the safety of the set and pursue his love in a real world—he will go and find Lauren, a girlfriend from earlier on in the show.

Morpheus's explanation in the *Matrix* (1999) of the power of question would have helped Truman. In one of the pivotal scenes in this film Morpheus says to Neo:

> You're here because you know something. What you know you can't explain, but you feel it. You've felt it your entire life, that there's something wrong with the world. You don't know what it is, but it's there, like a splinter in your mind, driving you mad. It is this feeling that has brought you to me. Do you know what I'm talking about?

As a young University student I sensed that there was something wrong with my world. While I could not put my finger on it, I knew that it was there. In time it would become a splinter in my mind and at times I felt it could drive me mad.

In her first years of school Carmen, our first-born, had the delightful ability to create new words. She once combined "difficult" and "struggle" to form the word *strugglety*. It was the word she created as she wriggled in her chair to do her homework and faced a second grade teacher who was keen to see her medicated for being "too active." I was tempted to use Carmen's word to describe the battle that erupted in the corridor between my head and my heart after the crashing of cars and the Soweto Uprising. But, as much as I love the word "strugglety," it would not begin to describe the ache I felt when I realized that the splinter in my mind not only distorted my vision of the world, it also caused a hardening of my heart and that my relationship with God suffered.

Divided Mind and Heart

The battle for the human soul is won or lost in the space between the head and the heart. As a boy born in the 1960s, I grew up in a world designed and controlled by apartheid: the stage was set, the matrix was in place. My dad started his career on the gold mines of Johannesburg. As the hoist driver he was the person who daily lowered big, black, African miners kilometers underground. It was here that I first met Africans. I have early memories of noticing how strong and imposing these miners were and, even when they smiled with brilliant white teeth, it evoked fear in me—as my mother clutched my hand.

In time my father's career advanced and we moved to the suburbs west of Johannesburg. These were happy days. Although my parents and most of my family agreed with and supported the Nationalist Government, they were Pentecostals. In this respect we were outside of the mainstream Afrikaner churches that, in many ways, were viewed as chief custodians of the Afrikaner identity and calling.

I remember many conversations and debates with school friends about doctrines like charismatic gifts, believers' baptism, election, and predestination. From a young age I was passionate about what I believed and my mind was my weapon of choice. My passion did not always keep up with my ability to explain my faith though. Many times I found myself retreating into this stance: "you may take away everything, but you will not be able to change my mind; I know what I experienced." At this time there was an apparent alignment between my head and my heart.

It was quite a simple theology that I was willing to defend: God is holy and we are not. We have sinned and God is willing to let his son die for us—he pays the penalty for our sin. In response, we put our faith in the son of God and through this personal faith we are saved. As a public declaration of faith, you *get baptized by immersion in water*, and the sin problem is solved. But not really. In addition you need the Holy Spirit as a second baptism to ensure that you *remain* holy. But, if you begin to sin again and you quench the Holy Spirit's work in your life, you will quickly find yourself slipping down a slippery slope to hell. And if you are in this backslidden state at the second coming of Christ, or you die while you are in this state, you stand no chance of making it to heaven. So, the only way to avoid this tragic outcome is to try harder. Do your best to live a holy life (don't drink, smoke, dance, go to the movies, and so on) and respond as often as you can to altar calls, where you can receive prayer and further deliverance from sin. But my Calvinist friends had a different view: God determines everything; humans have little choice since God elects some and rejects others; and the elect could not lose their salvation.

Altar calls were heart-wrenching, tear-jerking occasions. The pastor was small in stature but he was dynamic when he prayed for those who came to be delivered. Imprinted on my memory is the image of his hand on someone's head, the veins bulging in his neck as he called on God to bring deliverance. That head was often mine; I needed prayer more often than most. There were always olive oil and tissues available. One was used to invoke the Spirit's presence, and the other to deal with the nasal consequences of the Spirit's work.

If I could have my childhood over, I would not choose another church. It was a great community of people who were serious about God and loved each other. It nurtured me, and I was given many opportunities to develop as a young leader. At the age of twelve, the pastor called me to his office and he began to mentor me to preach a sermon on Psalm 121.

> I lift up my eyes to the hills—where does my help come from? My help comes from the Lord, the Maker of heaven and earth. He will not let your foot slip—he who watches over you will not slumber; indeed, he who watches over Israel will neither slumber nor sleep. The Lord watches over you—the Lord is your shade at your right hand; the sun will not harm you by day, nor the moon by night. The Lord will keep you from all harm— he will watch over your life; the Lord will watch over your coming and going both now and forevermore.[1]

I had just turned thirteen when I preached this sermon to a congregation of five hundred people. But even this text seemed to contradict the teaching that one could easily lose one's relationship with God. That God is ready, willing, and able to send those who backslide on a nonstop train to hell. My heart said: "No, God will never do that," but my head said: "You don't mess with a holy and anger-prone God."

Mind on a Quest

At age eighteen, I found myself ready to respond to what I believe was God's call on my life to become a pastor. Giving up my dreams to be an engineer, I set off for the local university to study theology.

Within months my life was turned on its head—I discovered I could use my brain to think my own thoughts. I was enrolled at the university in a pre-theology course. Within days, I was swimming in a sea of new ideas coming to me in lectures about ancient Israel, Babylon, Persia, and Greece. Over time, I began to think thoughts in Greek and Hebrew, and became conversant in theology, linguistics, philosophy, and psychology. The Bible was being studied like any other book. We were introduced to the original languages of the Bible, and I was obliged to read Scripture critically for the first time. Instead of a devotional reading of the Bible, I now had to

1. Ps 121:1–8 (NIV).

apply the historical-critical method of interpretation as well as structural analysis, form criticism, and literary analysis.

These new tools slowly eroded the fragile exterior of my childhood faith. Well-meaning professors, who were more interested in scholastic ability than spiritual experiences, challenged the theological certainties of my childhood. The tension between my head and my heart increased daily as the soft underbelly of my theological innocence was exposed. I simply did not have the ability to handle these new questions and I began to live a double life.

If only I knew then that what I was going through was well documented and recognized by others. John Westerhoff describes my experience in 1976 as "searching faith." It occurs when, through a personal search for truth, we move from reliance on the beliefs of significant others to self-sufficiency and individuality. It is a quest that ultimately enables personal ownership of and responsibility for beliefs and practices. But to get there the quest will require deep doubts, questions, and a willingness to test what has been handed down to us.[2] I was on a faith quest, a mind quest, but I did not have the tools for it.

On Sunday, our fiery pastor would use scare tactics; waving Scripture in our faces like a big stick. From Monday to Friday the image of God wielding a stick faded from my memory, and dry rationalism explained all the reasons for holiness away. There was no speculation, no allusion; everything could be explained, reasoned out, analyzed. In this modernist academic environment, even God had to fit into our neat boxes.

I soon became the pastor's principal critic; always ready to offer what I thought was constructive criticism on his exegetical methods. Only he knows where he found the grace to deal with my youthful arrogance. I certainly had none. My double life became even more extreme: youth leader over weekends, resident skeptic and budding agnostic during the week. I was even prepared to entertain thoughts that maybe the God of my Sunday school was just another god, like Zeus and the rest of the Greek pantheon.

My thought life was slowly crumbling; the naïve Pentecostal faith of my childhood could not stand against the relentless onslaught of new ideas and persuasions that university life brought. I was facing a faith crisis, but more accurately, I was coming out—out of my mind. The constructions that enabled me to make sense of my world up to this point had become restrictive and I needed to get out.

2. Westerhoff, "Journey."

During this period of my life, a bishop from Johannesburg, a so-called Communist and troublemaker, came to my university as a guest of David Owen, the foreign minister of England at that time. I think that Desmond Tutu, a black man, was only allowed to address us because the university authorities knew that it would cause an international outcry if he were denied the opportunity to speak.

My curiosity got the better of me and I went along to hear Desmond Tutu speak. To be honest, I was going to be part of those who would make it hard for him to speak. This was university after all, and here we test ideas. But behind it was a different motivation: I wanted to see just how inferior black people are to us.

By that stage Friedrich Nietzsche's Übermensch philosophy had begun to dominate my thinking. His ideas about the absence of God in life resonated with my experience of God at that time. If God did not exist, or even if he was dead to us, as Nietzsche argued, then we could not be certain about anything, including morals or values. The Übermensch will act as his own God, giving himself morality and value as he sees fit. Ultimately, the Übermensch rules over those who can not rule over themselves, and this, I thought, was the role of Afrikaners in South Africa.

Attending the lecture by Desmond Tutu would be the first time in my young Afrikaner existence that I heard a black man say more than, "Yes, sir," or "No, sir." While I had an African nanny for most of my childhood (and she said more than that, a whole lot more) black men were an enigma to me. The only black men I knew were those who helped us when the garden needed a strong hand, and those tall, menacing looking miners who I encountered in the mining complex we lived in for the first five years of my life. They frightened me, and apartheid ideology kept that fear alive in me for many years.

So, it was with some fear that I walked into the lecture hall where Bishop Desmond Tutu was to speak. My feelings were mixed: on the one hand I was excited, but on the other hand I felt like I was about to do something really, really bad.

Tutu's speech was electrifying and annoying all at the same time. He was short of stature, but a brilliant and prophetic speaker. When students tried to shout him down, I found myself siding with those who wanted to defend him. He was nothing like an Übermensch, he revealed a deep sense of calm in his relationship with God. He did not share our angst or our uncertainty about the existence God. As one who had experienced suffering and poverty, who had experienced oppression and dehumanization, God was still real and God's love for all people, black or white, was beyond question for him.

In that room, the black bishop from Johannesburg was the incarnation of Christ, and we, the white young elite who were mocking him, were the worst expression of the Übermensch—not even Nietzsche would have approved. For three years I had been in this space between the beliefs that had been handed down to me and a faith I could call my own. But now, for the first time in a long time, I felt again that I could believe in the reality of God.

When I try to remember what he said, I cannot. What caused the shift for me was not the words he spoke, it was not even what he did later in his political career. It was his courage to stand up against the powers that dehumanized him. It was his heart. I did not know it at the time, but Tutu's lecture, and perhaps even more so, his being, created a fresh link between my head and my heart. I felt the painful sting as my head and my heart made a first tentative connection, as the re-integrating my head and my heart began. Soon after this, Nietzsche's *Thus Spoke Zarathustra* dropped off my reading list and disappeared from my bookshelf at home. Tutu's life became a significant catalyst in my spiritual journey. But the journey had only just begun.

Heart on Display

A few years later in the early 1980s, Marian, my young bride, and I set off for the far-away land of America. We ended up in a small town in the southeast of the United States of America, 121 miles away from Atlanta, Georgia. South Africa was in the icy grip of international sanctions, but somehow I managed to obtain a scholarship to study overseas. What I did not know before we arrived there was that my scholarship would provide just enough money for my tuition fees. I would have to work as a janitor to pay for my books and housing in a trailer park.

It was in this trailer park that we came face to face with poverty for the first time in our lives. With not even enough money for food and electricity, life was hard. The snow that reshaped the landscape was beautiful at first, but then the harshness of the winter cold turned fantasy into misery. My days were filled with seminary lectures and my nights with completing research papers in English (my second language) and working as a janitor.

What was I thinking? What was God thinking—if he was there at all? "This is how one goes mad," I often thought.

Early on, I met Cornelius Ugandele from Uganda. He was a fellow student and a janitor on the same shift that I was. He was nothing like Bishop Tutu. Night after night Cornelius and I shared the same shift. Night after night we ignored each other, or at least I tried to ignore him. I was troubled by this situation. He was from a subordinate class of humanity, and here I was sharing a shift with him. What had I become? In the months that followed, my heart hardened as I continued to wrestle with my theological doubts and my nationalistic identity.

In the summer of my first year at seminary, I found myself in another unbearable housing arrangement. Robert Crick, the Dean of Field Ministry, decided that doing a basic quarter of Clinical Pastoral Education[3] would save my seminary career. In a conversation with him and a young, politically radical pastor from Atlanta, I was told that I would find myself back on a flight to South Africa if I was unwilling to address my lack of personal integration.

It was obvious to them that I lived "in my head." My analytical skills made me a successful student in subjects that required them, but Crick saw through me. "All head," he said, "and no heart."

Deep down I knew that he was right. I knew that I was unravelling emotionally and mentally. During this time I had a recurring dream. My older brother would perform open-heart surgery on me. After removing my heart from my chest, he placed it in a vice-grip. He worked feverishly on it while I shouted from the bedroom: "Hurry up, I'm turning blue. I am dying!" It was a sign that it was time for radical action. I was losing my mind, but I also knew that I needed to get out of my mind. I had to face my growing doubt.

3. This is how the Seminary describes the Clinical Pastoral Education (CPE) unit: "By arrangement through the Counseling Office, accredited programs in Clinical Pastoral Education (CPE) are provided on an individual basis. The CPE quarter generally runs twelve (12) consecutive weeks of full-time study in a clinical setting which offers peer group interaction, intense involvement with persons in crisis, inter-professional reflection and analysis, and individual supervision. Interested students must be screened and approved through the Association for Clinical Pastoral Education screening process. A debriefing process which reflects on the CPE experience in relation to their Pentecostal heritage and faith will be required of all students at the end of this training." http://www.ptseminary.edu/cat/fullcatalog.pdf, accessed February 13, 2013.

Marian was not allowed to join me in Atlanta, leaving me without emotional support. The next three months would be some of the most difficult months of my life, but they would change me forever.

The Clinical Pastoral Education program is probably the most intrusive theological process I can imagine anyone could experience. We were a group of about twenty students from many different religious backgrounds—Methodists, Baptists, Episcopalians, and other varieties of Christian tradition. All of us, each at different places and stages of theological development, were placed in small reflection groups. We were also assigned to a supervisor whose job it was to prod, push, and pull until there were signs of spiritual integration.

Once a week I would meet with my supervisor. He was a deeply principled man with great understanding of the human quest for truth, but also of the human fear to deal with it when it is surfaced.

I was assigned to a general ward, a children's ward, and also another ward for more serious illnesses. Every week we would spend time with patients and their families. Day to day, I would see people who were diagnosed with ordinary ailments as well as people who had exotic diseases. All of a sudden, life appeared a whole lot more fragile than I had understood.

We would write word-for-word accounts, called "verbatims," of the conversations we had with patients.[4] Every one of us would then be given a chance in a reflection group to present our verbatims. During these sessions, the other members could ask any questions, explore the style of care you provided, and reflect on what you included or excluded from your verbatim. It was often what was not said that drew the supervisor's attention.

I quickly caught on to the process and often found myself in the role of spiritual detective, prodding and pushing everyone except myself. Perhaps I was trusting that the best form of defense was attack, but my life began to unravel quickly.

One hundred and thirty-five miles away, Marian became very ill. I returned for a weekend visit, only to find her delusional from a raging fever. In a desperate state I rushed her to the emergency room at the local

4. Douglas R. Wilson explains that: "The verbatim traces its beginnings to the 1920s when Anton Boisen introduced the case study as the written human document for theological reflection. Boisen developed a detailed template of the information that needed to be gathered about a person. The strength of this tool was its ability to help students learn how to reflect theologically about the human condition. It did not address the pastoral skills of listening and intervention." In "Virtual Learning Seminar," CASC, accessed February 14, 2013, http://www.spiritualcare.ca/resources/virtual_learning.html.

county hospital where she was left unattended for hours while we waited for a specialist. She drifted in and out of consciousness. I really thought that my young wife would die that night, and then something remarkable happened: her fever broke and a deep peace entered the room. I do not have many stories of miracles to tell, but if asked, I would tell of what happened at Bradley Memorial Hospital. I still felt that life was fragile, but maybe God was real after all.

Splinter in My Mind Revealed

Back in Atlanta, life in our "rat hole" was not great. Our accommodation was in the attic of an old church. Apart from the single bed with a few missing springs and a stained foam mattress, I had no other luxuries. When I first arrived, my roommates (or fellow roof rats, for that is what we would become for the next three months) greeted me. One of them was Cornelius Ugandele, my co-janitor at Seminary, and the other was David Bryan, a suave West Indian.

I will never forget my first night with them. As I have mentioned, I come from an Afrikaner home and there my mother's standards for hygiene were equaled only by my father's ability to keep his garden in an immaculate state. I acquired this trait of my mother through osmosis and certain forms of child labor that were lawful and well within the parameters of Afrikaner parenting.

It was apparent that Cornelius and David must have had a very different upbringing. With great delight, they placed before me what appeared to be a freshly plucked chicken on rice. I was certain that the bird was still capable of laying eggs. It was, however, not so much the chicken that repulsed me, it was the eating utensils. All I could think was how they had been in an African or West Indian mouth before mine. I know this sounds pathetic, and I agree now that it is, but at the time I was having a personal crisis of apocalyptic proportions. I could feel the hot sweat gathering under the thin white skin on my forehead. Their eyes were burning on me, burning through every layer of my racial prejudice. The next three months were an unending scrutiny of our racial differences and biases.

My racism was also soon to be exposed at Egleston Children's Hospital. Over the years, as I have reflected on this story I am about to tell, I have had to drop my head in shame because I do not remember the name of the boy who changed my life. He is in many ways nameless to me, but for some reason I have chosen to remember him as James.

James was the child of an alcoholic mother and, as a result, acquired fetal alcohol syndrome. I was told that alcohol is a *teratogenic* drug, that is, it can cause serious birth defects in some children whose mothers ingest alcohol during pregnancy. He displayed the classic symptoms of this dreaded syndrome. His face and head were severely malformed and he suffered from mental retardation. The term *teratogenic* comes from the Greek word for "monster." James was the Quasimodo of the ward, and I had to care for him. As much as his malformations disgusted me, matters were only made worse by the color of his skin. He was a black boy. Deep down, in my twisted thinking, I concluded that this little boy was suffering like this because black people were all the same: they needed Europeans to take care of them.

Working in the children's ward was very difficult for me. How do you have a good theological conversation with children anyway? Give me the angry Portuguese mother of six whose husband had just been diagnosed with incurable pancreatic cancer and I could take her on theologically. "What kind of God do you represent?" she asked, before confessing that she was the slut and the one that God should punish. She was relentless in her grief and guilt: "My husband is good. He is at Mass every week. I should die, not him." This was my kind of intellectual challenge; an opportunity to try my latest theological insight, but hide emotionally. It did not work with her, by the way, and my theological prowess was even less effective with children.

When James was around, my job would become even harder. His little face was without a nose and his mouth was always half open and dripping with saliva. The truth was that my standards of hygiene, which were so lovingly instilled in me, and my own compulsions to be clean would not allow me to touch most people, let alone James.

But, on a destined day, James and I met in the long and wide corridor of the Egleston Children's Hospital. There was an electric storm outside and James, frightened by the thunder, came out into the corridor. I was surprised, even shocked, by his presence. Before I could do anything, a petrified, slobbering, shaking, little black boy was holding on to me. Many thoughts flashed through my mind, but to my shame the dominant thought was that I needed to get him off my clean pants. My disgust for the little boy and for all that he represented crashed to the surface.

I managed to get him back onto his bed, still doing everything in my might to free myself from his desperate grip. As I peeled his last finger from my arm he swung around, now clinging onto a stuffed toy animal. His eyes became cold and I looked away. It was what Charles Gerkin, a practical theologian at Chandler Theological Seminary, called an "opportune moment," a window when an opportunity for transformation opens up.

James's action exposed me. I felt deeply ashamed—ashamed of my inhumanity. This boy, who needed a human to hold him and love him, found in me only disgust and an inability to respond with compassion or affection. If the result of his mother being addicted to a teratogenic drug was that it produced a "little monster," then surely my motherland, the land of my birth, was also on drugs to have produced me.

I was so locked up in my own mind of racial prejudice that I could not even compete with the stuffed toy animal. I knew then that I was a prisoner in my own mind. To be free, I needed to get the splinter out of my mind.

I left his room, my heart exposed. I cried freely for the first time in many years.

3

Anxious Minds

Sin in Soul and Society

The days immediately following my encounter with James are a blur in my mind. I was afraid, falling apart (and the irony is not lost on me) as I took anxious steps toward discovering who I really was.

As I began to recover from the immediate emotional impact of my encounter with James, I was left with a deep thirst to know the other side of the South African story. Chandler School of Theology was on the same campus as Emory University Hospital, where I was doing the Clinical Pastoral Education. They have a magnificent library called the Pitts Theology Library. In its basement I discovered papers that would have been banned in South Africa in those days. These papers told the story of the cruelty that was being perpetrated in the name of God. I could not believe what I was reading and seeing. I realized that this was not a perfect society and that there was a separation that cut even deeper than the one I had feared as an Afrikaner. Sometimes I would hold fragile photocopies of photos in my shaking hands, stunned by the story they told of government brutality and murder. Now there was no doubt in my mind that people were suffering in South Africa, even while I was reading these sacred documents. I was horrified to discover that the perpetrators of this violence were people who looked like me, who spoke my language, and who sang the same songs in worship.

For the first time in my life, I was ashamed to be an Afrikaner.

One of the many myths I studied as part of the Classical Greek course that I was introduced to during my undergraduate program is the story of Prometheus. Prometheus was the creator of human beings and he tried to advance his creation, but Zeus had no interest in the mortal race of humans. He was content for humans to live as primitives until they all died off. Prometheus, whose name literally means "forethought," could not accept this. He set out to trick Zeus by giving the mortals assistance and knowledge that had been hidden from them. The last straw was when he gave them fire in their dark caves. This infuriated Zeus and he had Hephaestus shackle Prometheus to the side of a cliff high in the Caucasus Mountains. There Prometheus would hang until the anger of Zeus subsided. Each day, Prometheus would be tormented by Zeus's eagle as it tore at his immortal flesh and tried to devour his liver. Each night, as the frost bit its way into his sleep, the torn flesh would mend so that the eagle could begin anew at the first touch of dawn.

In retrospect, I can see how the Greek myth of Prometheus could not have been far from my mind at that time. It vividly depicted why I object to the notion of a God who is perpetually angry. Prometheus risks the wrath of Zeus to help humans. In the Christian story, Jesus plays the role of Prometheus. He attempts to save humankind; because he sees our potential he is willing to risk his life and face the wrath of God, his Father. But look at what that got him: the cross. Jesus endures our separation from God, his Father, by becoming separated himself. While this helped me appreciate Jesus more, it also raised many more questions about God as Father. How could I believe in a God who would see another suffer so that his sense of justice would be satisfied? That view of God created the mind trap that encaged me for most of my childhood; the same view that was used as justification for apartheid and many other atrocities committed in the name of Christianity. I needed desperately to be out of this mind trap and experience a renewing of my mind.

Anxiety in Soul

Pitts Theological Library also introduced me to Paul Tillich. He was a theologian who wrote most of his theology before and after the Second World War; he reflects on the human plight of separation. Tillich argues that the fundamental issue facing humanity is the possibility of *non-being*, or our mortality and possible annihilation. After the fall, human beings, who once lived in intimacy with God, found themselves in a world where they were separated from God.

Tillich describes God as the *ground of being*.[1] For him, God is the seedbed, the deepest reason for human existence. As a result of the fall, human beings have been separated from this ground of being and we have become deeply anxious about the prospect of non-being.

Humans thus face one basic threat—the possibility of non-being. This is our deepest and ultimate concern, says Tillich. This concern is experienced at a universal and personal level. At a universal level we are threatened with the total extinction of being, with nothingness as our final destiny. At a personal level, we are threatened with personal mortality. Tillich would say that we suffer from the loss of being what we were created to be and of becoming what we were supposed to become.[2] The anxiety that marks human existence is the result of our separation from God.

We were not created to be separated from God—the ground of our being. We have been hardwired for intimacy and for relationship. We feel anxious because we have been lifted from our ground of being. We are not close to the bosom of the one who created us; our anxiety is the result of separation. At Egleston Children's Hospital my encounter with James exposed the true nature of my anxiety.

The Christian story as told by Tillich and others does not suggest that separation is a normal part of human existence. The story of how human beings were created tells us that we were created to be intimate with God—Genesis chapters one and two tell us this with great insight. This is the real "normal." We read in chapter three, however, that things changed; they became abnormal. A serpent enters the story and suggests a way of living that is separate from God. It can be said that the serpent introduces the notion of separation—separation between God, others, and creation—a life that is essentially selfish.

I find it interesting that the Greek word for the personification of evil, as seen in the devil,[3] can literally be translated as "to pull apart or render asunder." This seems to me to be the fundamental work of evil in the world. To pull apart what once was united. To bring division where there once

1. Tillich, *Courage to Be*, 157.

2. Ibid., 44–48. Also, Tillich distinguishes three types of anxiety: "that of fate and death (ontological), that of emptiness and loss of meaning (spiritual), and that of guilt and condemnation (moral)" (ibid., 41).

3. *Diabolos* is a Greek word often used to point to the personification of evil in the world.

was unity. This is exactly what the story in Genesis tells us. As soon as evil entered the human story, disintegration became part of the human fabric. Our human experience is thus one of longing for integration, which is really a longing to be reunited with God, although we do not recognize it as that. The Christian journey is towards an integrated life with God, self, and others.

More recently, this point was beautifully illustrated on a television show. The program investigated the strange pets that people have in contemporary Australia. This show was about piglets. The presenter picked up a little piglet, but the squealing of the piglet was so ear piercing that the presenter nearly dropped it. "Hold it close to your chest," the owner instructed. As soon as the presenter obeyed her, there was a thankful silence. Then the owner explained that the little piglet associates that kind of lifting with death. In the wild, if she was lifted up like that it would probably mean that a bird of prey had grabbed her and was taking her to the nearest tree. Piglets do not like being lifted off the ground; it makes them anxious.

Anxiety in Society

With the help of Tillich, I can see that it is also true for all of human life. It is a positive statement about the human longing for union. Psychologically speaking, the word union may suggest wholeness and healing. Under the "Separate but Equal" policy of apartheid, union was only permitted within racial boundaries. But beyond race, anxiety expressed in separation, segregation, and fragmentation were the hallmarks of life in South Africa.

For those of us who were born and nurtured under apartheid in South Africa, the notion of segregation summed up this anxious way of living. It was etched into our collective subconscious as a holy and fundamental principle of life. To question this principle, as I had begun to, was tantamount to questioning God and finding fault with how he had determined things to be.

Life in this mechanical system was about boxes and rules. There were rules that determined what went where, labels that gave worth or demeaned individuals and groups of people. As a white boy, this was my understanding of things: stick to the rules, the way things were meant to be, and life would be good.

In retrospect, it seems quite plausible to argue that the apartheid system was designed to keep *white anxiety* at bay. During nearly fifty years of rule in South Africa, the supporters of apartheid wanted to secure a perfect society; a society where everyone had a place determined by God, where everything worked according to its design and function. For myself, as an Afrikaner, this society had always seemed to work like a well-oiled machine; every part in place, doing its job, moving us forward. In order to make this machine work, to keep everything in its place, people had to be classified. This classification determined where you could live, what kind of education you could receive, what function you could fulfil in society, what you would be paid, with whom you could socialize, and whom you could marry. As I reflect on this, the South Africa of my childhood, I can appreciate an ironic twist.

The apartheid system in South Africa was a cocktail of laws. Very strict and discriminatory laws controlled basically every aspect of life; they even determined the boundaries of families. In the early days of apartheid, it was even possible for families to be divided along color lines.

Anecdotally, a family could arrive at some official government office to experience a race classification procedure. One might expect that this classification procedure would involve some medical procedure. Not so. Instead of a medical doctor, a government clerk would apply two administrative trials: the pencil and the fingernail tests. Every family member's hands would be inspected to see if there was any hint of blue in the fingernail bed. If your fingers had a European pink tinge, you could still fail the pencil test. A pencil was inserted in to the applicant's hair and if the pencil stayed in your hair because your hair was too curly, you failed the test to be classified as a European. Those who were classified as non-European would lose their rights, property, and significant relationships, even if other family members were classified as European. No wonder that those who lost their "European status" often spent the rest of their lives in a battle to regain this.

To be declared white was to join the Afrikaner dream, even if you did not speak Afrikaans. Black South Africans wanted to take this world away from us, we were told. And then there were the friends of the black South Africans: the Communists. They were atheists, opponents of Christ, and eager to get access to the rich mineral resources of South Africa. This was all to advance their godless mission in the world, the state propaganda declared. The apartheid laws, Afrikaners believed, stood between life and death, being and non-being. We feared that our society would fall apart, that we would lose our perfect existence, and so our leaders introduced more classifications, more laws, clauses and sub-clauses to the Constitution, and South Africa became more segregated—and more anxious.

Sin in Soul and Society

As I came to terms with all of this in the Pitts Theological Library, I also had to face the truth that South Africa's sin was my sin. While societies give birth to individuals and we are shaped by these societies, we are still free to choose how we will live. I needed to understand this anxiety that held so many South Africans and me in an iron grip for decades. Paul Tillich's sermons[4] helped me understand the link between our individual sin and the sin of our societies.

While I did not have Ted Peters's *Sin, Radical Evil in Soul and Society*[5] in the Pitts Theological Library, this book has in the last decade helped me to frame the conclusions I came to then. I share his view that we all carry an anxiety within us, and that this leads to sin in soul and society. Anxiety is not sin; anxiety is amoral. It is how we choose to manage this anxiety that matters. Peters says that we have two options in response to this dilemma: faith or unfaith.

Faith is about trust. It is to return to the ground of our being, as Tillich would say. The story of the little piglet I told earlier illustrates the point. Unfaith, on the other hand, is the first step towards sin. Unfaith is to take matters into our own hands because we want to ensure that our lives amount to something. It is an interesting observation that unfaith can often masquerade as faith. I hear this so often when Western Christians quote what they believe is in the Bible: "God helps those who help themselves."

According to Peters, pride is the first evidence of unfaith. Instead of trusting God, we place our trust in some other object or person. As a young South African, I grew up believing that God was at the center of our society; that we did put our trust in God. Today I hold a very different view. It seems to me now that in apartheid South Africa we worshipped the idea of a nation that was called to a new land. Our nation was our pride. We took matters into our own hands to ensure that it became what we believed it should be; what we believed God ordained it to be.

As a young boy I often sang the South African anthem with great pride. Even now, as I write these words, I am aware of the impact this song has had on me:

4. Tillich, *Shaking of the Foundations*.

5. Peters, *Sin*.

Ringing out from our blue heavens,
From our deep seas breaking round,
Over everlasting mountains,
Where the echoing crags resound,
From our plains where creaking wagons,
Cut their trails into the earth,
Calls the spirit of our Country,
Of the land that gave us birth.
At thy call we shall not falter.
Firm and steadfast we shall stand,
At thy will to live or perish,
O South Africa, dear land.[6]

At the heart of what we really believed as Afrikaners, then, is that it was the land that gave us birth, that called to us and gave us the strength to continue. It was also the land that could ask for the ultimate sacrifice. This land is what we lived for as South Africans under apartheid. In fact, it was really the land that gave us security. I see now that our trust was misplaced.

Along with this misplaced trust in the land, South Africa was introduced to the notion of concupiscence. This is a very old English word. Its root meaning is "desire," but more generally it is to want what others have. In the most basic sense, concupiscence manifests in sexual lust. Peters explains it like this: "More generally concupiscence is the desire to acquire, to own, to indulge, to take pleasure, to consume. It causes us to covet and disposes us to greed and avarice."[7] Fundamentally then, concupiscence is a perversion of love. If love is the ability to be real and to be intimate, then concupiscence destroys and inverts that. Concupiscence points to the separation between human beings. In our anxious rush to secure our own human survival, as if that is ultimately possible, we will take from others what is not ours.

In our day and age concupiscence is perhaps best seen in our consumer mentality. We have even coined a term for it—retail therapy. The issue here is that we go beyond simply buying items that we need and are often spending money that we do not have. I think that concupiscence creates the kind of hyper-reality that was first described by the French philosopher Jean Baudrillard, and more recently explored by Umberto Eco. Hyper-reality is a state of being where we are no longer satisfied with the real. We are only satisfied with the "authentic fake."[8] This was life under apartheid too.

6. *Die Stem*. Words by C.J. Langenhoven, melody: Rev. M.L. de Villiers.

7. Peters, *Sin*, 125.

8. Eco, *Travels in Hyperreality*; Baudrillard, *Simulations*.

Concupiscence is not only a problem experienced and faced by individuals—it also besets societies and nations. Peters says:

> Capitalism depends on the production of what Karl Marx called surplus value, the excess value of profit that results from the production of goods. Surplus value is tied up to freedom—or so we have convinced ourselves. The greater our ability to control and reinvest surplus value, the more freedom we have. Marx identified the desire to gain control of the surplus of others as the primary drive between classes and between nations.[9]

In an apartheid South Africa the surplus value was eventually possessed and controlled by the small white minority. Over the years, as I have reflected on my life, I have had to come back to this reality: my education and so many other immeasurable advantages in my life are the direct result of the benefits of our Afrikaner concupiscence.

Self-justification follows short on the heels of concupiscence. In essence self-justification is a web of lies that we tell ourselves. We know deep down that concupiscence will not work; we know that ultimately we will die and our effort to take life from others will come to nothing. Peters explains it like this: "In order to maintain the illusion that concupiscence will in fact succeed, we invent lies—lies that identify us with what is good. Sometimes these lies identify some others as evil, justifying the conclusion that they should die and we should live."[10]

For so many years I had identified myself and my people with what I believed was *good* in this world. Those who disagreed with us, especially black South Africans, were identified with *evil* and were deserving of what they were getting. Self-justification is identifying oneself with the good. Scapegoating is identifying others with evil. They are like two sides of a coin.[11]

The Afrikaner interpretation of Calvinist theology provided the perfect frame of thought to achieve self-justification. We believed as Afrikaners that we were God's elect, those he had predestined to be his tribe in Africa. God had given us the land to be his people. In this view of God, Afrikaners found the perfect alibi.

When we wilfully use our power over others to inflict pain or to maintain control over them, we move from self-justification to cruelty. Up to

9. Peters, *Sin*, 128.

10. Ibid., 161–62.

11. Ibid., 162.

this point we could perhaps have claimed to be ignorant of the impact that our pride, concupiscence, and self-justification had on others. But once we move on to cruelty we are crossing a line. We can no longer claim to be ignorant of the effects of our actions on those who are our scapegoats. "The suffering of others works like a drug; the cruel person needs increasingly larger doses to attain the same high. The ultimate fix is the death of the other,"[12] says Peters. It seems to me that he might even be right when he invokes the Lifton principle: "Killing others relieves our own fear of being killed."

The next step is blasphemy. We blaspheme if we destroy the means by which someone else can experience grace. "Blasphemers," says Peters, "tarnish the name of God to the point that people no longer think to call on it to ask for divine grace."[13] Normally we would associate blasphemy with using God's name inappropriately. While I can understand that using God's name in vain is blasphemy, it is ironic that we can be cruel and even torture people in the name of God—even claiming to do this as an act of worship.

As I said earlier, today the irony is not lost on me. I believe that most of what we did in the name of apartheid was blasphemous. With the wrong view of God, our actions became blasphemous. No wonder many turned their backs on God and the church. This is why Desmond Tutu is a hero in my eyes. He is a man who, in the darkest days of apartheid, stood against the blasphemy that rolled off the lips of the priests of apartheid.

After a very long, dark night of the soul, I finally emerged from the basement of the Pitts Theology Library like Jonah from the stomach of the big fish that swallowed him. I was reborn with a desire to make peace with God, others, and myself, but this would not be easy. It would require a whole new mind.

12. Ibid., 194.

13. Ibid., 17.

4

Mind Quest

Making Up My Mind

I was ill-equipped to deal with the new uncertainties that flooded my mind, my thoughts, and my feelings as I returned from Atlanta and my encounter with James. The church has generally been suspicious of the place of questions in the life of believers. Very little time, if any, is devoted to constructive teaching about the virtues of questions. Fortunately, back at the seminary after my stay in Atlanta, I discovered a community that understood the pedagogy of the Spirit and the place of questions. While I appreciated the deposits of faith from my childhood, I knew that it was time to make up my own mind. The Seminary was the ideal place to do that. In this community I learned that if Christ could spend an anguished night in prayer, if Jesus could cry out from the cross, "My God, my God, why have you forsaken me?" then surely I am also permitted to ask because I do not understand.

Making Up My Mind

If we are denied the freedom to find out what we think and how we feel about it, if we are denied the freedom to make up our minds, if we are not free to question the incongruencies of our lives, we will soon find that faith produces dogmas and not vibrant beliefs, pragmatism and not thoughtful actions. When we are not allowed to claim personal ownership of and responsibility for thoughts and feelings, then I believe our minds and faith are being colonized.

Colonized faith will no more tolerate questions than a bird keeper obsessed with locks and keys tolerates an open cage. It is possible that one could question just for the sake of questioning, but what I have in mind here is the appreciation of the place of questions in sparking faith-quests, the appreciation of the place of questions in pointing to humility in thought, as a willingness to admit that we might not be seeing the whole picture, or not be seeing it clearly. David Dark describes this kind of questioning as sacred. He writes, "When we're exposed to the liveliness of holding everything up to the light of good questions—what I call 'sacred questioning'—we discover that redemption is creeping into the way we think, believe, and see the world."[1]

Questioning can be dangerous, but then most things in life that are worthwhile contain some element of risk. The only way forward is to face our questions, to handle our questions like an experienced electrician would handle an electric current—with caution. In this way, the freedom to question becomes a gift to explore and a way to gain a holistic understanding of the conditions of our existence.

For faith to remain alive, it needs to follow the movements and contours that are God in human history. Guder reminds us that:

> God's mission unfolded in the history of God's people across the centuries is recorded in Scripture, and it reached its revelatory climax in the incarnation of God's work of salvation in Jesus ministering, crucified and resurrected. God's mission continued then in the sending of the Spirit to call forth and empower the church as the witness to God's good news in Jesus Christ. It continues today in the worldwide witness of churches in every culture to the gospel of Jesus Christ, and it moves toward the promised consummation of God's salvation in the eschaton ("last" or "final day").[2]

If in our faith journey we ignore the unfolding story of the mission of God, our theology becomes *caged*, which will lead to stagnation and ultimately some form of death.

In recent times, Michael Frost and Alan Hirsch expressed their fear that this has already happened in parts of the church. They introduce their

1. Dark, *Questioning Everything*, 14.
2. Guder and Barrett, *Missional Church*, 4.

readers to two very powerful images of stagnation: the billabong and the tidal pool.

A billabong is an Australian term for a pool of water that once was part of a river or a creek, but which has been cut off from the flow as the river slowly changed direction. Many second and third generation Christians find themselves in a church billabong. Where once their parents were part of a church that was like a flowing stream, now they are trapped in a stagnant backwater.[3]

The second image comes from the ocean.

The church ought to be like a tidal pool rather than a billabong. In the deep rock pools created by the ever-swirling surf of the ocean, whole ecosystems can develop filled with weed, rock crabs, molluscs, etc. If left untouched by the ocean, the pools would overheat in the sun and become stagnant as the sea life dies. What a tidal pool needs is the regular flushing of the ocean as the tide rises and falls, sweeping the pool clean each day.[4]

This is so true for human life as well. If there is no room for fresh water to flow, we become stagnant or we overheat in some way, destroying life. This is the kind of stagnation that I experienced in apartheid's system and the caged theological system that supported it.

Today I believe that it is more helpful to look for answers and not find any than it is to be given answers. In this place of tension, where questions resist easy answers, questions will lead to a quest, says Brian McLaren.[5] Parker Palmer encourages the seeker to embrace the tension of unresolved questions because the tension itself pulls the heart and mind to be open "to a third way of thinking and acting."[6] Pursuing sacred questions, I discovered, does not necessarily destroy faith and truth, but rather it can be the key to a beautiful mind. A mind that is free to inquire, integrate, and to innovate.

Inquiring Mind

Michelangelo Merisi da Caravaggio, an erratic follower of Jesus in the Roman Catholic tradition and a famous painter, was troubled by many

3. Frost and Hirsch, *Shaping of Things*, 85.
4. Ibid., 86.
5. McLaren, *New Kind of Christianity*, 4.
6. Palmer, *Hidden Wholeness*, 175.

questions. As a Catholic believer he was caught in the aftermath of the protestant reformation of the sixteenth century. Caravaggio, the man of contrasts, lived in a world of extremes. His parents lived through the violent times of the Protestant Reformation. As a young man he would have been aware of the strains caused by the Reformation and Counter-Reformation.

He will not be remembered, though, for his fascination with physical violence or for his desire to shock. Perhaps more than anything else, Caravaggio is remembered for the use of dramatic light and shade in his paintings—a painting technique called chiaroscuro. I believe this is an element in his work that suggests that he understood something of the struggle that we as humans have with shades in life.

One of my favorite paintings is his depiction of the Doubting Thomas.[7] This painting more than any other has fascinated me for many years now. This painting is pregnant with meaning. It opens a window on a private moment between a disciple who lost his faith, and a risen Christ who never gave up hope. The dark shadows and vivid contrast of light employed by Caravaggio has given me permission to call into question, to wonder, to even be petulant, knowing that Christ will not leave the room.

I think this is how Caravaggio lived, between the extremes of black and white. He was not a man of moderation. His life story, which is well documented, reveals how he would dedicate himself for months to his craft. During these times he would produce some of the most beautiful works of art. Then he would leave his studio for months, going from one social event to the other, always armed and ready for a fight. Finally this way of life caught up with him and he killed a man in a brawl. With a price on his head, he fled Milan only to die a few years later.

It is in this world, where Roman Catholic and Protestants were locked in a battle of life and death, that Caravaggio painted *Doubting Thomas*. Thomas was not present when Christ first appeared to his disciples after his death. When the other disciples told him that they had seen Christ, he refused to believe it until he had seen and touched Jesus's wounds for himself. When Christ reappeared, this time in Thomas's presence, he invited Thomas to explore his wounds. Caravaggio captures that moment brilliantly like no one before or after him. He captures the moment when Jesus not only invites Thomas's questioning, but also sanctions it. Jesus allows questions.

Painting Thomas has been a popular theme in Christian art from the fifteenth century onwards, but no one painted Thomas's inquiring mind

7. Dated 1602–1603.

as well as Caravaggio. In most of these paintings, Jesus seems distant from the *nuisance* of the inquiry imposed upon him by his unbelieving disciple. Consider, for instance, the painting of Hendrick ter Brugghen,[8] a contemporary of Caravaggio (see below). He seemed to miss the main drama and consequently he depicts Jesus as moody as he endures Thomas's investigation.

In contrast, in the painting by Caravaggio (see below) we see Jesus assisting Thomas as he inserts his index finger into the gaping wound in the side of his master. After many visits to this picture, I noticed the importance of light and shade in this account of the events.

Jesus, who is standing on the left, is fully in the light. Another disciple is placed immediately behind Thomas on the far right. He is completely in the dark. It is as if Jesus and this disciple are in contrast—Jesus has the answer and this disciple is still wrestling with questions.

Thomas is in the front and center. His forehead is in the light and his exploring hand shares the light with Christ. His hand and the guiding hand of Jesus are completely in the light. But more than this, Thomas's hands seem somewhat enlarged like the hands of a laborer. Worship and work have the same roots in the Greek language—could it be that this inquiry is to be seen as an act of worship? Could be that loving God with all our minds, means that we ought to have an inquiring mind?

8. *Incredulity of St. Thomas* (c. 1621–23).

A third disciple stands at the back between Jesus and the other disciple. We cannot see much of him as Jesus, Thomas and the second disciple obscure his body. The striking feature of this disciple is that he seems older than the other two and his head is completely enlightened. It is as if to say, "I understand this." This disciple gets it.

Jesus, as I already pointed out, is in the light: he represents the truth of the Christian story. The disciple on the far right is in the dark: his mind is still filled with questions. The disciple in the top of the picture is the most enlightened disciple: he has explored the questions and answers and he is satisfied with the content of his faith. His head shares the light with Thomas and Jesus. But Thomas is still putting the theory to the test—the wounded Jesus was dead, but now he is alive. As I was recording my observations—and I do not claim that this was Caravaggio's intention—I noticed that the light reveals a pattern that graphically illustrates the tensions that I think we face in everyday life; a tension that creates a vortex in which we seek meaning. The kind of vortex I found myself in after my encounter with James. This is a picture of faith seeking and constructing meaning.

If it were not for Jesus's willingness to be the subject of scrutiny, then these men would all have been in the dark. Asking questions, as I came to understand, does not mark the end of faith, it signals the intention to seek meaning.

Integrating Mind

I have observed that life seems to make sense when we engage the tension between what we believe and the ways in which we express our faith in action.[9] Humans seek to make sense of life in this tension between theory and practice. This need to make sense of life, to understand life, seems to be at the heart of theology. Anselm, the medieval Bishop of Canterbury, described theology as "faith seeking understanding."[10] For him, believing matters of faith and theology preceded understanding. After we believe, reason ought to be applied to gain a deeper intellectual understanding of the things we already believe. In other words, belief is both logically and chronologically prior to reason, but faith includes both belief and reason.[11]

If faith seeks to make sense of the incongruence between theory and practice in the midst of a changing world, then faith is more than a noun; it is a verb. Faith enables action in a world that has been shaped by the stories that we have learned and embodied. But it seems to me that faith also needs to makes sense of the tension between traditional answers and emerging questions. A simple diagram will illustrate the demands placed on the theologian by these tensions (see diagram below).

9. This tension is expressed in Latin *fides quae* and *fides qua*. I will not persist with the Latin phrases. From here on I will refer to this tension as the tension between theory and practice. The Latin phrase *fides quae creditur* points to the content of faith, "that which is believed." I use it here to point to the "What of faith." Latin phrase, *fides qua creditur* points to the character of faith that is apprehended. I use it here to point to the "How of faith." It can also be translated as, "that faith by what is believed."

10. It is interesting that in addition to *fides quae* (theory) and *fides qua* (practice), faith can also be described as *fides quaerens* when *quaerens*, the Latin word for "search" or "hunting," is combined with *fides* (faith) and *intellectum* (understanding). Anselm of Canterbury introduced the theological word to this motto, *fides quaerens intellectum*, "faith seeking understanding."

11. See Grenz et al., *Pocket Dictionary*, 52.

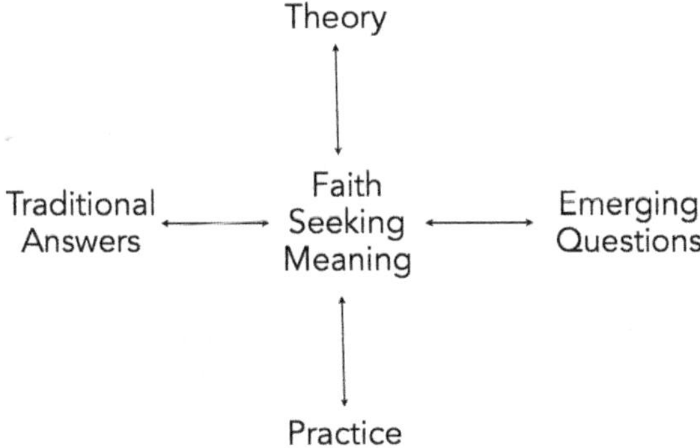

Where these intersect is where we experience the greatest amount of tension. It is the place where Thomas's finger penetrates the wounds of his teacher and friend; it is the place that Jesus willingly opens for Thomas to explore. Here is where Thomas will find the *splinter in his mind*, the one that has been driving him mad. This place can be the place from which meaning will emerge. The sustained tension of this *quadpolarity* creates a context of ideas and questions in which we can seek and find meaning.

This, then, is the function of theology for the believer: to enable meaning-making in the context of everyday life. It enables faith that endows life with meaning.

It was in James Fowler's *Stages of Faith: The Psychology of Human Development and the Quest for Meaning*,[12] that I first encountered the idea that faith could be more than doctrines or practices, that it could be the human activity of meaning-making. Four years before this insightful work, Fowler had already indicated that he was more interested in the form or structural characteristics of faith as knowing, and that the content of faith was not his primary concern. He said that his research team was looking at faith as a way of knowing and interpreting rather than that which is known or interpreted.[13]

In order to understand what Fowler means by faith, we must be alert to the distinction he makes between faith and belief. In essence, Fowler sees faith as a worldview—the way in which we view and give meaning to life. In his words, it is the most "fundamental category in the human quest

12. Fowler, *Stages of Faith.*

13. Fowler, "Perspective on Faith," 211. Here Fowler speaks of "knowing and construing."

for meaning."[14] His model also describes faith as an expression of how we holistically understand the conditions of our existence.

Belief is different for him; belief points to the content of our faith, the doctrines that we hold to. Belief is more *theory* while faith, for Fowler, is *our attempt to seek and construct meaning*. Faith, then, seen from this perspective is:

> A disposition of the total self to the total environment in which a trust and loyalty are invested in a centre or centres of value and power which give order and coherence to the force field of life, which support and sustain (or qualify and relativise) our mundane and everyday commitments and trusts, combining to give orientation, courage, meaning, and hope to our lives, and, to unite us into communities of shared interpretation, loyalty, and trust.[15]

What Fowler is suggesting is that all human beings have faith. This faith is the lens that we have crafted for ourselves to give meaning to life. At the center of our faith is an integrating motif or principle, which he calls a "center of value and power"; the centripetal force that I referred to earlier. This integrating principle holds it all together for us. If we combine Fowler's insights with our understanding of the centrality of story in the human quest for meaning, then we can easily conclude that story is the medium through which our "center of value and power" is shaped and transmitted.

Innovative Mind

I am not surprised that Lloyd Alexander concluded that "we learn more by looking for the answer to a question and not finding it, than we do from learning the answer itself."[16] I know that I am not very comfortable with living in the grey uncertainty of unresolved questions. Living with unresolved questions is difficult. My impatience demands an answer, a resolution of the issues, because I want to live in certainty. Sometimes it seems that I

14. Fowler, *Stages of Faith*, 14.

15. Fowler, *Trajectories*, 137. In Dykstra and Parks, *Faith Development and Fowler*, 25, he defines faith more technically as: "The process of constitutive-knowing underlying a person's composition and maintainment of a comprehensive frame (or frames) of meaning generated from a person's attachments or commitments to centers of supraordinate value which have power to unify his or her experiences of world thereby endowing relationships, contexts and patterns of everyday life, past and present with significance."

16. Alexander, *Book of Three*, 9.

might even be tempted to settle for a quick superficial answer to avoid the discomfort of living with unanswered questions.

I once saw a poster in a church hall that read, "To every question there is an easy answer, and it is normally wrong." Can it be that in our search for immediate and absolute certainty we are too willing to close ourselves off to questions that will require a patient pursuit? Is that perhaps why we give in to the addiction of instant gratification as we settle for superficial platitudes? We thus miss the opportunity to find answers that are marinated over time in the deep human search for meaning. Is this how we miss out on true happiness? It seems that if we do that, we have settled for second best, and that we do not really have a longing to know.

That the human search for answers requires a mind that longs for meaning is illustrated for me in the Walt Disney movie, *The Little Mermaid*. My daughters and I were often transported to an underwater sea kingdom ruled by King Triton, ruler of the seas. The king's daughter, Ariel, is fascinated by human life, so she wants to go to the surface and find out for herself. Sebastian, the crab, the undersea conductor of the royal orchestra, tries to convince her not to go. In the famous song *Under the Sea* he sings: "The seaweed is always greener in somebody else's lake. You dream about going up there, but that is a big mistake. Just look at the world around you, right here on the ocean floor. Such wonderful things surround you. What more is you lookin' for?" Sebastian knows that there is a longing in this little girl that will not easily be silenced.

C. S. Lewis identified this longing as central to the human quest—the longing for more. He explains it like this:

> Creatures are not born with desires unless satisfaction for those desires exists. A baby feels hunger: well, there is such a thing as food. Men feel sexual desire: well, there is such a thing as sex. If I find in myself a desire which no experience in this world can satisfy, the most probable explanation is that I was made for another world.[17]

Ariel wants answers about the outside world and explores ruins of human ships underneath the sea for treasures. She takes whatever she finds to Schuttle, the seagull, so he can tell her what they are used for. Schuttle does not really know anything about humans and he confuses a fork (or what he calls a dinkelhopper) with a comb. Her hunger for more and her impatience with superficial or misguided answers from Sebastian and Schuttle

17. Lewis, *Mere Christianity*, 121.

motivate her to push through the pain of not knowing until she finally finds herself sitting at a table with humans. There she sees a "dinkelhopper" and combs her hair with it! It may be true that her longing for more leads her to this embarrassing place, but it is also true that it helped her to discover a truth far more mysterious than the use of human utensils—she discovers love. She finds a truth that would transform her life.

As we set out to ride a bicycle for the first time it is a bit overwhelming. We question our ability, our equipment, and especially the one who is pretending to hold the seat while we set out on our first adventure. Fear can even overtake us as we imagine the worst thing that can happen—the dreaded first fall. And as certain as I am of my breathing as I write this sentence, sooner or later it happens. There is crying and ointments for the broken skin and ego, but, because we want the adventure and are motivated by our longing for the freedom that the newly acquired skill will bring, we persist. In time we become more confident on the few centimeters of inflated rubber and we learn to go with the flow. We learn that when we fall to the left, turning the wheel into the fall is far better than resisting it. We learn that momentum is our friend and that when you think about falling too much, it is likely to happen.

Etched into my memory is the delight on my daughters' faces when they realized that they were cyclists. With great delight they called: "Look dad, I can do it!" And I quietly thanked God that they were safe and that they have adventurous minds. I think that it is the same when it comes to learning to live with questions. We come to realize that questioning is a normal part of life. It becomes as natural as breathing; to avoid questions is to settle for training wheels.

In the so-called developed world, however, we do not forever use bicycles as our main means of transportation. Our vehicles of transportation become more complex and require even more skill. In the same way, as we progress through the stages of life, the questions of life become more challenging. Brian McLaren picks up on this reality when he describes life as a journey with many stages along the way. In *Doubt: The Tides of Faith*, he says:

> I call the first stage simplicity, where everything is simple and easy, black and white, known or knowable. Then there's complexity, where you focus on techniques of finding the truth—since the scenario has gotten more complex. Then there's perplexity, where you become a kind of disillusioned learner, where you doubt all

> authority figures and absolutes, where everything seems relative and hazy. I used to call the fourth stage maturity, but a friend pointed out it would be better called humility, because in stage four you come to terms with your limitations, and you learn to live with mystery, not as a cop-out, but as an honest realisation that only God understands everything. You carry out of stage four a shorter list of tested and cherished beliefs that you base your life on, and a lot of your previous dogmatisms are now held more lightly. In a sense a person keeps finding faith and then becoming frustrated with it and in a sense losing it, and then finding a better version of it, and so on, maybe like a software upgrade . . . [18]

Oliver Wendell Holmes Jr. a justice of the United States Supreme Court made a telling comment a century ago when he said, "I would not give a fig for the simplicity this side of complexity, but I would give my life for the simplicity on the other side of complexity."

Whole New Mind

Under the careful theological guidance of the seminary faculty, I became more and more willing to stand outside of beliefs that I inherited as a young Afrikaner; I developed the skills and the appetite to scrutinize, abandon, or embrace some of these thoughts and feelings.

Questions, I now believe, are inherent to how we thrive as humans in this world. The Christian story reveals that even in the perfection of the Garden of Eden, these questions were aired by humans who could not see the future, and whose design as human beings required that they foster their relationship with the Creator. Since God alone is able to see the past, present, and future—and can do this all at the same time—they needed his perspective. They shared in his most beautiful mind. While humans were in an unspoiled relationship with God, their questions were sacred; they were part of worship and work in the Garden of Eden. After this relationship between God and his image bearers was spoiled by unfaith, the human limitation to see only in part became the Achilles heel of human existence.

We experience the present as a product of our history and we anticipate the future in the light of what has gone before. And, as we do, we ask questions all the time. These questions may be as elementary as: "What will

18. McLaren, "Doubt," accessed February 17, 2010, www.brianmclaren.net/emc/archives/resources/ doubt-the-tides-of-faith-written.html.

happen next?" Or more profound and daunting as: "Why did this happen?" Or, "Why did God . . . ?" We cannot see around corners and we certainly cannot look ahead into time. We cannot even know what will happen in the next minute or the next second. It is even harder to see in non-physical ways. Much of life is unpredictable or uncertain simply because we have limited vision in so many ways. It is because of this limited vision that we have to learn to live with questions. It is human privilege to ask if we do not understand, and it is only a tyrant who will deny us this human pleasure.

In the story that followers of Jesus find themselves in, humans are once again able to enjoy a personal relationship with God. So much so that their lives are hidden with Christ in God, says Paul. A closeness that humans once had, but that was lost in the Garden of Eden,[19] is a possibility again. Paul knows full well that Jesus promised his followers, then and now, that they would not be left alone and without answers to questions. Jesus promised that his successor, the Holy Spirit, would lead them into all truth. This surely implies that the disciples would have doubts, would ask hard questions, but that the Holy Spirit, as a master teacher, would use human uncertainty as an opportunity for growth in knowledge. This is how sacred questions lead to conversion in the true sense of the word—a change of mind.[20] We receive the potential for a whole new mind.

In my pre-seminary days I believed that to question was to doubt, and to doubt was to be unbelieving—so it was better not to question. The church under apartheid in South Africa seemed to have all the answers. It was "simplicity on this side of complexity"; it was to live my life with training wheels attached to my mind. After my encounter with James, and as I wrestled through the dark night of my soul in Atlanta and began to experience the pedagogy of the Spirit, the training wheels came off and I could appreciate the place of questioning. As I now stand outside of beliefs that I had inherited as an Afrikaner, I am able to scrutinize, abandon, or embrace them. I am able to mind the gaps in my thinking, especially my view of God, that shaped my spiritual formation as an Afrikaner boy. I am ready to ask hard questions about God and the authority of Scripture in my life. This is what we will turn to in the next two chapters.

19. See Colossians 3:1ff.

20. In Biblical Greek *metánoia* literally means "a change of mind."

5

God Minding

Finding Peace of Mind

Even though I had a scholarship to study theology when we went to the United States of America in the early 1980s, I did not really want to know God. I was only interested in the intersection between psychology and religion and knowing about God would be an academic exercise at best. The sentiment of Teresa of Avila summed up my spiritual condition. She prayed, "Oh God, I don't love you, I don't even want to love you, but I want to want to love you."

To secure their colonialist aims it was very important for the engineers of apartheid to call on a God who was distant and scary. The God of the Old Testament, who was capable of extraordinary acts of violence, fitted this prerequisite well. The Old Testament images of a God who was angry and stern suited the faceless men of apartheid because he could exact the same revenge on those who disobeyed the God-appointed rulers of the land. As an aside, I now understand that misinterpretations like this illustrate why we need a consistent approach to interpretation that references the whole Bible and not only selected sections.

I was a boy of sixteen when Steve Biko,[1] a Black Consciousness leader in South Africa, was tortured and murdered by the South African government. I have a vivid memory of being in the backseat of our family car when the radio announced that Biko had died in prison. Even then I found

1. He was the founder and martyr of the Black Consciousness movement in South Africa.

the reaction of James Kruger, the South African Minister of Police, jarring. He said: "I am not glad and I am not sorry about Mr. Biko. It leaves me cold."[2] The apparent coldness of the Minister of Police would not attract the wrath of the god of apartheid, but rather his praise.

Gaps in Mind

There were major gaps in my knowledge and experience of God by the time I became a seminarian. Initially, it did not matter to me that God had favorites among the nations—this helped to explain why Afrikaners were so special. I could read through the blood-drenched pages of Leviticus and Judges and conclude that the nations are in God's hands and that he can do as he pleases. Black people, as the descendents of Ishmael and Esau, were paying the price for the sins of their forefathers. But it still did not make God likeable or lovable to my mind. The God of the Old Testament appeared to be an unpleasant, bloodthirsty despot over nations. His actions seemed capricious, his attitudes towards sin, petty, and his outbursts of anger reminded me of the malevolent schoolyard bully that I often faced.

After my experience with James in Atlanta and the discoveries I made in the basement of the Pitts Theological Library, this picture of God became a theological chasm that I had to cross; it was the ultimate gap I had to mind. Even though I was studying theology at that stage, I did not love God; I did not even like him.

While this view is primarily based on Old Testament readings, the New Testament did not provide much comfort at this time. While I still did not resolve the conflicts I had about the God of the Old Testament, I now also felt an intense desire to understand why God would allow his son to be tortured on a cross. How could God the Father turn his back on the bloody figure of his son on the cross? And, just to complicate matters even further, during this time Marian and I lost our first child late in her pregnancy. The question became even more personal.

Even though I had received most of my theological training in some of the best universities in South Africa, and even though I was raised in a Christian environment that believed in the Trinity, I had a firmly entrenched patriarchal view of God. In that view, fathers have the last say. To me this meant that one could argue that God the Father wanted his son to

2. *Rand Daily Mail*, September 14, 1977.

take the fall for him, and that is what happened. But this view did not satisfy me anymore.

How could this God who confronted my racism in Atlanta be so cruel towards his own son? In my early reflections on the cross, God the Father's seemingly aloof stance reminded me more of the older brother than the loving father in the parable of the prodigal son. How could God the Father be so loving towards us and yet discard his son on the cross? How could a father who truly loves, abandon his son in his hour of need? Did Jesus not cry, "My God, my God, why have you forsaken me?"[3] This gap seemed impassable to me.

If God could allow his son to be tortured while he retreated to the safety of his throne room, could he then not be doing the same with all human suffering? Did he condone the torture of those who fought apartheid in South Africa? Or was it simply that the image of God being aloof and distant from the suffering of his own son had become my model for my own distance and aloofness when I was confronted by torture and other acts of inhumanity? These gaps had to be closed in my mind so that I could know him and love him.

Minding the Dissatisfaction Gap

Very soon after my encounter with James, I stumbled upon a very important Old Testament Scripture that went a long way to changing my view of the God of the Old Testament. This is a text that records the words of God to the people of Israel while they were still in exile, years after the Babylonians had taken them from their homeland. The prophet Jeremiah records these words: "The Lord appeared to us in the past, saying: I have loved you with an everlasting love; I have drawn you with loving-kindness."[4]

This Scripture speaks of a kind, merciful, and faithful God who pursues with passion and determination those whom he has created. It became evident to me that this Scripture reveals a God who knows rejection—the very beings that he created can, and do, reject his love. If this were not true, then why would God have had to pursue them? He was, however, neither deterred by their juvenile behavior nor repelled by their misbehavior.

3. Matt 27:46 (NIV).

4. Jer 31:3 (NIV).

According to this passage, God loved them with a love that was stubborn and kind. The Hebrew word used for "love"[5] here has caused many translators sleepless nights. Most translations create a double-barrelled English word such as "loving-kindness" to convey its full meaning. On the one hand, the word refers to stubbornness—the persevering nature of the one who loves. On the other hand, it refers to kindness and compassion.

When we put these two words together we are reminded of the picture that Rembrandt painted with so much care and beauty. The hands of the father are both stubborn and caring, but more about this later.

This passage also speaks about how God "draws"[6] Israel, and therefore humanity, to himself. The Hebrew word that the prophet chooses to describe this action of God also emphasizes God's determination and perseverance. This word points to God's determination to woo us. God is determined to integrate our lives with his own, to bring us back to himself.

The Hebrew word for "draw" can also be translated as "to lift out" and it reminds me of another very beautiful image of God's love in the Bible. In Psalms 18, the Psalmist speaks about a personal crisis that he once experienced. He was, perhaps, walking one day in a dry ravine, unaware that there had been a storm higher up in the mountains. Before he knew it, the ravine turned into a river in full flood. The waters swept him off his feet and he was dragged downstream. The debris that the rushing water had collected along the way was attaching itself to him, weighing him down. From time to time, he would make it to the surface and cry out to God. Just as he was about to give up, a hand grabbed hold of him and flung him out onto a rock. He was miraculously rescued. He realized that God drew him, lifted him out; that God heard his cry and rescued him. With his chest still burning from his near-death experience, he announced that God "brought me out into a spacious place; he rescued me because he delighted in me."[7]

The word "delight" is a wonderful word in Hebrew. It is one of the love words of the Old Testament. Love has many sides to it, as we all know, but this word refers to the joyful element of love. The joy that two young lovers experience as they discover their love for one another; the joy in

5. The Hebrew word *hesed* can be translated with the following words: goodness, kindness, and faithfulness. While it is often translated as "loving kindness," it can also be translated as "mercy."

6. Hebrew *mashak*: to draw, lift out, to sow, to sound, to prolong and to develop.

7. Ps 18:19 (NIV).

holding your child for the first time, it is a joy that turns us in-side-out and up-side-down.

It has been many years since my mind first noticed the gap in my knowledge of God. Slowly but surely, as I am minding the gap between the god of apartheid who is an unpleasant, bloodthirsty, despotic, capricious, and malevolent schoolyard bully, and the ambidextrous, *hesedic*, *maskaking*, delighting God of the Bible, I get glimpses of a loving creator who calls me his beloved. Our creator is not a Zeus-like being who later regrets that he made. Instead, we were created out of the love of God to be the focus of his affection, his collaborators on earth in whom he delights.

The German mystic Meister Eckhart once said that God created out of the "laughter of the Trinity." This explanation of the origin of the human race sounds far more appealing to me than other popular ideas. This seems to narrow the gaps in my mind.

Minding the Hierarchy Gap

At seminary, this hierarchical view of God came under new scrutiny. My search for answers took me to the Cappadocian Fathers who, as brothers and friends, provided the earliest explanations of the Christian doctrine of the trinity.[8] I had noticed that C. S. Lewis and others often found their answers about God there. Perhaps I would too. These early church leaders used, among many technical terms, the word *perichoresis* to describe God. I will persist with this Greek word because I think that it is central to the point I am trying to make. Volumes have been written about this and I will not pretend to be a specialist on this subject, but that does not diminish the impact that the notion of *perichoresis* has had on my theological formation. The Greek *perichoreuo* means to "dance around." Like so many Greek verbs, this is a compound verb—two words making up one new word. The verb *choreuo* is "to dance." When it is joined by the preposition *peri*, which means to "encircle" or "encompass," it closely resembles *perichoreo.*

Theologians have been intrigued by this word for years. For instance, Thomas Torrance suggests that it points to a "dynamic three-way

8. Two brothers, Basil the Great (AD 330–379) and Gregory of Nyssa (AD 330–395), and a close friend Gregory of Nazianzus (AD 329–89) became defenders of Nicene orthodoxy and carried forward the work of Origen, Tertullian, and Athanasius in formulating the doctrine of the Trinity.

reciprocity" between Father, Son, and Spirit in what he calls "the *perichoretic* co-activity of the Holy Trinity."[9]

In speaking of the Trinity, Miroslav Volf explains this doctrine more carefully: "In every divine person as a subject, the other persons also indwell; all mutually permeate one another, though in so doing they do not cease to be distinct persons."[10]

This description reminded me of the musical smash hit *Riverdance*. "What do you get when 80 of the most talented Irish dancers and musicians are joined by the incredible vocal styling of Brian Kennedy? A night on Broadway that you'll never forget!" This is how it was advertised on the internet.[11] One of the outstanding features of *Riverdance* is that if you were to look through the narrow slit in a large piece of cardboard at just one of the eighty dancers, you could just as well be looking at all of the dancers on the stage. They dance in perfect unison. On the other hand, were you to look at all of the dancers at once, you would see them as if they were one person.

The Cappadocian Fathers had a more substantial view of the Holy Spirit than the one I had held as a Pentecostal boy and that we can learn from *Riverdance*. They described the Holy Spirit as the personification of the love between the Father and the Son. Stanley Grenz gives a good account of this:

> The bond between the Father and the Son is the mutual love they share. Throughout all eternity, the Father loves the Son, and the Son reciprocates that love. Out of love, the Father generates the Son, and the Son in turn reciprocates the love of the One who generates him.[12]

Grenz helped me to see that love describes God's inner life. Millard Erickson agrees,

> They are bound to one another in love, agape love, which therefore unites them in the closest and most intimate of relationships. This unselfish love makes each more concerned for the other than for himself. There is therefore a mutual submission of each to each of the others and a mutual glorification of one another. There is complete equality of the three.[13]

9. Torrance, *Christian Doctrine*, 198.

10. Volf, *After Our Likeness*, 209.

11. http://www.briankennedy.co.uk/riverdance.html.

12. Grenz, *Theology*, 74.

13. Erickson, *God in Three Persons*, 331.

God is therefore a being who shares life, who is in his very essence a community; a God who creates out of the overflow of his being and who calls his creation to participate in this shared life. Clark Pinnock writes, "By the Spirit we access the presence of the Father through Jesus Christ." When this happens, we "are swept into a divine world of mutual love and begin to experience the very goal of our nature as spiritual and social beings."[14]

Minding the Judicial Gap

Through the eyes of the Cappadocian Fathers and with the able assistance of theologians such as Torrance, Pinnock, and Grenz, my dominant view of God as an inflexible prosecutor, jury, and judge is melting away. And in its place a fresh, hope-filled question has emerged: Could it be that God is more interested in overcoming alienation and enslavement than he is in being judicially satisfied? The perichoretic view of God pointed me to something beyond justification and penal justice; it suggests that there is more to God than a mere thirst for retribution.

The way I think about this now is as follows: if it is true, as Paul says, that the same Spirit that raised Jesus dwells in us,[15] and if we share the same Spirit, then this Spirit binds us to Jesus and we, with Jesus, have an intimate personal relationship with the Father. Paul's description, "For you died, and your life is now hidden with Christ in God,"[16] makes a whole lot more sense to me now.

I no longer see the Spirit's main aim as being to hand out spiritual goodies. Rather, the Spirit wants us to be bonded with the Son and to join the dance that is the community of the Trinity itself—to join the mission of God as he makes the world a better place. Pinnock writes, "Spirit is leading us into union—to transforming, personal, intimate relationship with the Triune God."[17] This suggests that there is more to Christianity than sinners being saved from sin and God's sense of justice being satisfied. Through what we have called salvation, God transforms human beings so that through his Spirit we have the mind of Christ; we are capable of communion with God.

14. Pinnock, *Flame*, 38.
15. Rom 8:11.
16. Col 3:3.
17. Pinnock, *Flame*, 149.

To use the categories of Irenaeus, we move from being simply the *image of God* to becoming the *likeness of God.* Humanity is important to God—the God of the Christian scriptures is not anti-human after all. Pinnock would argue that we share this bond with all humanity through the unity that the Spirit provides.[18]

This mutual permeation, this mutual dependence, is a picture of the true intimacy that exists within the Godhead. For the first time it occurred to me that God as Father, Son, and Holy Spirit were all involved in the plan for Jesus to lay down his life. The cross could then be a sign of God's willingness to risk life and limb to restore the intimacy that was lost in the fall.

Some of my earliest memories are of waking up under a church pew during mid-week Pentecostal prayer meetings. These meetings were emotionally charged and the Spirit's power was invoked through lengthy and passionate prayer. I viewed the Spirit as the person in the Godhead who enabled spiritual encounters. As a child I thought that if you lived a holy enough life and were clean enough, then the Holy Spirit would visit you and you would have an exhilarating emotional experience. But with this perichoretic understanding of God, I began to understand that God himself wanted to draw me into this eternal dance. He woos, he laughs, he dances—now I know: God wants me to join the dance.

Minding the Aloofness Gap

Jürgen Moltmann was not light reading for most seminarians in the 1980s. Nevertheless, it was his books, especially *The Crucified God,*[19] that began to defrost my perceptions of how God responded to the death of his Son—and how he would respond to the death of Steve Biko.

As soon as Moltmann became more intelligible to me, I realized that this German described God neither as angry and aloof nor as cold and calculated as he sent his Son to a cross. According to Moltmann, when God's Son cries out from the cross for help, he does not turn away from him as if to say, "I know it hurts now, but your pain will soon be over." I know from personal experience that I did not believe my parents when they said that spanking me hurt them more than me. The picture of God that developed through the writings of Jürgen Moltmann resonates well with what I later

18. Ibid., 117.

19. Moltmann, *Crucified.*

discovered in Clark Pinnock. It is a picture of the cross with not only Jesus hanging on it. Instead, it is a cross that holds the Trinity—Father, Son, and Holy Spirit.

Moltmann was one of the first post-war theologians to reflect on the graphic and horrific story that was told by Elie Wiesel.[20] It is about a young Jewish boy who was hung by the Nazis along with two other men in the camp at Buna. The boy did not die immediately; his death was prolonged by thirty minutes of suffering. The onlookers around Wiesel asked: "Where is God now?" Somehow Wiesel heard the answer coming from within himself: "Where is he? He is here. He is hanging there on the gallows." Moltmann comments with great insight and tender pastoral grit:

> Any other answer would be blasphemy. There cannot be any other Christian answer to the question of this torment. To speak here of a God who could not suffer would make God a demon. To speak here of an absolute God would make God an annihilating nothingness. To speak here of an indifferent God would condemn us all to indifference.[21]

If I could create a caricature of my pre-Moltmann view of events that led to the crucifixion of Christ, it would look like this: there is a throne room and God the Father is sitting alone. The place that Jesus once occupied is now empty and there is a sign that reads: "vacancy, apply within."

I do not hold to that view anymore. Elie Wiesel's picture of God is now closer to my way of thinking. When Jesus was here on earth there was no vacancy in God's being—the Trinity was still three in one. The Trinity was still a perichoresis. So, when the man Jesus died on the cross, the perichoretic union was turned into a dance of great distress—a funeral waltz.

What happened on the cross was the most extraordinary thing. God put his own existence on the line to achieve a new reality for humankind. We are well acquainted with Jesus's side of the suffering on the cross, but God the Father was suffering too. Maybe one day we will fully understand his pain. The relationship between Father and Son was stretched to breaking point. The Spirit, as the bond of love, was at pains to keep the Godhead from disintegration.

This was the darkest point in human history; this was the most dangerous moment in divine existence. What happened on the cross expressed

20. Wiesel survived Auschwitz, Buna, Buchenwald, and Gleiwitz. In 1968 he was awarded the Nobel Peace Prize.

21. Moltmann, *Crucified*, 274.

the most profound ontological threat to the Trinity. Jesus's death may not have been the death of God[22] as the God-is-dead-theologians contended in the 1960s, but it was the death in God.[23] There can be no more-profound description of despair.

But there is good news. God overcomes despair as the Spirit raises Jesus from the grave. The Bond of love turns despair into hope, the dark shadow of death into the light of the resurrection. Love wins. The resurrection is therefore as important as the cross in our understanding of what God did at Easter. This is the moment when God in himself overcomes despair. This is when Father, Son, and Spirit overcome the dark night of the soul and hope becomes available to all of humankind. It is as if, at this moment, God makes a statement about the significance of humanity. In Jesus, the statement is clear—humanity can overcome despair and doubt and be a vehicle for hope. Human life does not have to disintegrate; integration is possible. Defragmentation is not our ultimate destiny, even though it might sometimes look as if you are out of your mind when you are in fact trying only to make sense of life.

My sermonizing instincts take me back to what Paul said about us: "The same Spirit that raised Jesus from the dead dwells in us."[24] This means that I can finally make peace with God—he is not cold and aloof. He is more like the God that Shillito described in his *Jesus of the Scars:* "The other gods were strong, but Thou wast weak; they rode, but Thou didst stumble to a throne; but to our wounds only God's wounds can speak, and not a god has wounds, but Thou alone."[25]

Peace of Mind

Over time, my appreciation for what really happened on the cross has deepened and it continues to do so, and I have become more at peace with God as Father. While I do not claim that I know exactly what has occurred, I am confident that God put on display a love that is not easily expressed in English words. Rembrandt van Rijn chose to paint it in, *The Return of the Prodigal.*

22. Altizer and Hamilton, *Radical Theology*, 135.
23. Moltmann, *Crucified*, 243.
24. Rom 8:11 (NIV).
25. Shillito, "Jesus of the Scars."

Central to the picture is the prodigal son. The fact that the prodigal is dressed in his underwear reveals just how far he has fallen and how much disgrace he has heaped on his family. His under-cloak is in tatters and is stained yellow; no longer fit for human use. Rembrandt draws the attention of the viewer to the feet of the unfortunate young man. His one foot is out of his slipper, revealing the scars caused by an arduous journey; his other foot is still in a slipper but the slipper tells a story of misery and pain. The prodigal is a shadow of the man he used to be. He is undone.

His father stands over him dressed in a red robe. The robe and sloping posture of the father conjure up the image of a protective hen that is gathering her chicks under her wings. With his hands on his son's back, the father leans over the emaciated frame of his returning son, as if to cover his shame. It is clear that the father loves his son, who is kneeling in front of him. He is completely focused on him and totally oblivious to the judgmental gaze of his older son who stands to the right, aloof and distant.

While the whole picture has been an amazing source of inspiration to me over the years, it is especially the hands of the father that have captured my imagination. It was Henri Nouwen who first made me aware that there was something peculiar about the father's hands. Here are some of Nouwen's poetic descriptions:

> The father's left hand touching the son's shoulder is strong and muscular. The fingers are spread out to cover a large part of the prodigal son's shoulder and back. I can see a certain pressure, especially in the thumb. That hand seems not only to touch, but, with its strength, also to hold. Even though there is a gentleness in the way the father's left hand touches his son, it is not without a firm grip. How different is the father's right hand! This hand does not hold or grasp. It is refined, soft, and very tender. The fingers are close to each other and they have an elegant quality. It lies gently on the son's shoulder. It wants to caress, to stroke, and to offer consolation and comfort. It is a mother's hand. The Father's love is not just that of a great patriarch. He loves like a father as well as a mother. He holds and caresses, confirms and she consoles. That gentle caressing right hand echoes for me the words of the prophet Isaiah. "Can a woman forget her baby at the breast; feel no pity for the child she has borne? Even if these were to forget, I shall not forget you. Look, I have engraved you on the palms of my hands."[26]

As a child I was well acquainted with the god of apartheid South Africa, a god with only a left hand, but now I have been introduced to the God who has a left and right hand. After the foolish boy comes home from his season of self-indulgence and wild living, he does not find in his father a judge or an unpleasant professor of morality. Instead, he finds in him a hospitable host and carer. He finds a wedding planner, a disc jockey, a barman, and a chef. His father runs around to ensure that everyone is having a good time, that there is enough to drink and that the food is cooked to perfection. We see a picture of a delighted father who does not give up on those who do not want to join the party in honor of his son who was dead and is now alive. Celebration is the most natural expression of this father's joy.

Being a first-year theological student, and one who did not really like God, would send shivers down the spine of many admission officers. As it

26. Nouwen, *Prodigal Son*, 98–99.

turns out, my doubts and dislikes, my crisis of faith, were not an impediment at all. Instead, these provided a fertile environment for my theological studies, perhaps even more so than if I had started with no question at all.

6

Story Minding

Following the Trajectory

As my mind changed about God, I began to see that God the Father is not a distant and aloof despot that needs his wrath soothed by the blood of his son. I also needed to mind a second gap though: the authority of Scripture. As my thoughts and feelings about God began to change I noticed that the overall story of Scripture was also changing for me. It became the authoritative story of God's dealings with humankind, and I am invited to join his-story.

The big Story that we find ourselves in is that God wants humans to live this human life here on earth in union with him.[1] While we are living here and now, our lives are now already present in Christ in trinitarian life. To live this human life in union with God is the essence of the Christian story. It is the unfolding plot of the story that we find ourselves in. I began to see that more than doctrines and propositions, we live our lives through stories—unfolding narratives through which we are able to make sense of our lives.

Easter as the culmination of the biblical story is no longer just about my salvation and my way of getting to heaven. It is even more to me than satisfying God's need for justice. As we discussed earlier, this event *is* the earthly representation of the divine drama—when hope and new life overcame death in God. His ascension, which is part of the Easter events and is often ignored by many Christians, is just as important since it points to how

1. Richards, *Practical Theology*, 50.

our humanity is now present through Christ in trinitarian life. Through the man Jesus, humanity is now "hidden with Christ in God."[2]

When we speak of theology, we often think of it as a collection of doctrines or a list of rules that we have to live by. It is, however, stories that seem to be the preferred medium through which we are able to express the propositions of our faith and the actions that mark our faith. Through storytelling, we often generate meaning that enables us to live meaningful lives in a changing world. Since stories attempt to understand our situation (out of which questions arise), and since stories can demonstrate that our symbols and traditions provide faithful answers to emerging questions, stories function as theology and become custodians of *faith as seeking meaning.*

The movie *Big Fish* (2003) illustrates how stories can shape a life and how we are shaped by the stories we live in. Tim Burton of *Edward Scissorhands* and *Beetlejuice* fame is the director of *Big Fish.* Edward Bloom, the main character, seems to live a very ordinary life, but he is an utterly delightful master of detailed and fantastic storytelling. His son Will is, however, not impressed. He is frustrated to the point of hostility because he sees his father's stories as a web of lies. He cannot seem to get to know his dad; nothing from his childhood really makes any sense. In fact, he does not really know who he is as Edward's son.

When Will is told that his father is dying, he returns home to discover the truth to these questions of identity, integrity, and intimacy. This is not an easy task as his father stubbornly clings to his version of reality, which Will believes is a fantasy.

It is easy to understand why Edward's big fish stories are so important to him: they enable him to make sense of his life. As I watched this movie, I was amazed to notice how annoyed I became with Will's scepticism. I knew that Edward had created a flamboyant world, but his son's pragmatic approach to life was almost as unwelcome as his father's augmented understanding of truth. I observed how Will, the doubting Thomas in this story, attempts to sabotage his father's version of reality, and how close he comes to being the villain in the story. But the redeeming moment for me is when Edward is on his deathbed and Will is by his side. Edward cannot find rest; he needs his son to tell him the story of how it all ends. Will, in a moment of compassionate insight, understands his father's request; one by one he evokes the fictional characters that his dad introduced him to as a child, and all of them are there in Will's story as Edward is lowered into

2. Col 3:3 (NIV).

the river and gets away, like big fish do. Edward, the big fish, dies in peace. But in a final twist, at Edward's funeral we meet in real life the outrageous characters that featured in his tall tales.

For me *Big Fish* illustrates a point that Charles Gerkin once made:

> Language constructs worlds. To have a world, to live in a world, means for humans to inhabit a time and place in which a certain language is connected with experience to give meaning to that experience. More than anything else, to make meaning marks the human as human.[3]

Through stories we make sense of *who* we are, of *how* we are, and *whose* and/or *with whom* we are. This is just another way of saying that stories give us a sense of identity, they shape our integrity, and they establish our intimacies. We make up our minds about life through the stories that we tell.

As early as 1971 Stephen Crites made the now famous statement that "the formal quality of experience through time is inherently narrative."[4] It's impossible to identify ourselves, to describe what we experienced or what we mean, without telling a story. We create meaning as we build intrigue, develop characters, describe actions, and develop a plot that runs through it all. No wonder Crites concludes: "Stories, and the symbolic worlds they project, are not like monuments that men behold, but like dwelling-places. People live in them."[5] As we tell our stories we are attempting to create order and with order comes meaning. Walter Brueggemann was one of my favorite Old Testament theologians while at seminary. He also makes the connection between stories and meaning-making when he writes: "Our life of faith consists in moving with God in terms of (a) being securely oriented, (b) being painfully disoriented, and (c) being surprisingly reoriented."[6] The ability to tell stories is a uniquely human characteristic. Through stories we are able to place the different elements and experiences of our lives in their proper places.

In the same way, the Bible tells us a story. For Christians the Bible is the authorized biography of God's life in and among his creation. This biography is the authoritative collection of human stories that reveal how God engaged humanity and how different people responded to God; it is this story that we still find ourselves in, that is still unfolding. It can of

3. Gerkin, *Living Human*, 39.
4. Crites, "Narrative Quality," 291.
5. Ibid., 295.
6. Brueggemann, *Praying*, 16.

course be viewed from a distance, as we would view a mountain, but as a follower of Jesus the story is *our dwelling place*. Over the years I have come to appreciate that the Christian story contains three distinct sections, or movements. There are many different ways to describe these movements, but they are essentially created through two main events, or turning points.

It Is a Story of Generativity

The first turning point after creation is the so-called fall of humankind; the second is the death and resurrection of Christ. This leaves us with three movements, which Aida Spencer labels as "before the curse," "under the curse," and "beyond the curse." While I appreciate this approach, I find the language of "curse" quite confusing and negative. I want to propose an alternative and call the three movements: generative, de-generative,[7] and regenerative (see table below).

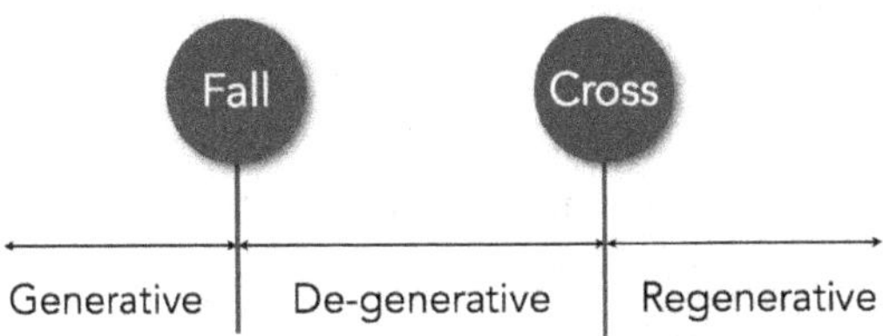

It is quite interesting that we get to know Adam and Eve as adults, and as adults they are generative. Generativity, according to Erik Erikson (1963), whose psychosocial theory of human development is still used widely today,[8] is the psychological showpiece of the mature human adult.

Adults, according to Erikson, construct an identity in adolescence, find intimacy in a long-term committed relationship as young adults, and then in adulthood, seek to make a positive contribution to the next generation. Among many other commitments, adults invest their time and energy in parenting, mentoring, teaching, caring, and leadership to ensure that their families, communities, and organizations will be sponsors of growth, development, and wellbeing in the next generation. Through these positive

7. My intention is not to use this word pejoratively; I am hyphenating it to speak of a situation that is steadily becoming worse.

8. See McAdams, "Explorations." And more recently, Wilt et al., "Eriksonian Developmental Scripts," 156–61.

activities and many more, adults become "stakeholders and destiny shapers in society."[9] They are being generative.

We could say then, that at first Adam and Eve had an adult caring relationship with God, with each other, and creation. They were generative.

In Genesis 1 and 2 humans experienced God's care and in turn and in response to God's mandate, they would take care of God's creation as generative beings—*stakeholders and destiny shapers in society*. Central to all of this is the idea that the story we find ourselves in begins with God's love that is generative. Rowan Williams once said, "In loving his own productive, generative, generous love, God loves all those ways in which that love can be realized in creation."[10] This *productive, generous love* spilled over into the creation of human beings. It is why we are image bearers of God. We were made to enjoy intimacy with God, with each other and with all of creation, as did Adam and Eve. We were created to be generative.

As a pattern for all human relationships, God revealed to Adam that a man should leave his father and mother and cleave to his wife and that they would become one flesh.[11] I believe the three actions in this imperative point to three vital elements in human relationships. It culminates in a beautiful word picture of generativity—*and they will become one flesh.* The oneness and yet differentiation within the trinitarian understanding of God in Christian scriptures is a model for human relationships. Let's have a closer look at these verbs.

Generativity starts with a decision to engage another person. A man leaves his parents to be present with his wife, to engage her as person of equal worth. It seems somewhat counterintuitive that we have to leave (be absent somewhere) to be present. But if we do not make the choice to leave a place, we cannot be present somewhere else. As humans we cannot be omnipresent, we cannot even be multi-present. But it is more than being physically present; it is about engaging the other person as a person. Engagement is the oxygen without which this relationship cannot breathe.

Generativity requires more than engagement; it needs trust. *Cleaving* in this text could point to *trust* as the second ingredient of healthy

9. Vaillant and Milofsky, "Male Psychological Health," 1348–59, cited in McAdams "Redemptive Self," 81–100.

10. http://www.brainyquote.com/quotes/quotes/r/rowandwil256097.html#i2wYvdvXeMEDQC7w.99

11. Gen 2:24 (NIV).

relationships. The Hebrew word translated as "cleave,"[12] literally means to adhere; to glue, to join, but also to follow closely. This reminds me of the great insight of the ancient wisdom writer who insisted that human relationships were designed to make us stronger, and that trust is the key:

> Two are better than one, because they have a good return for their work: If one falls down, his friend can help him up. But pity the man who falls and has no one to help him up! Also, if two lie down together, they will keep warm. But how can one keep warm alone? Though one may be overpowered, two can defend themselves. A cord of three strands is not quickly broken.[13]

In the richness of presence and the closeness of trust a new reality is generated—strands become a rope—there are no longer three separate strands, but a rope of three intertwined strands. The whole generated by the three strands is greater than the sum of the parts. The phrase, *they shall become one flesh* invokes images of weaving and braiding. While becoming one flesh speaks of a sexual union, there is more to the picture. It seems to suggest that as two lives are united through leaving and cleaving, they weave a new identity. Human relationships, when they are healthy, generate life that will outlast them. This is at the heart of generativity.

The relationship between the primordial man and woman gives us a pattern for all human relationships. To my mind, these three words—leave, cleave, and weave (see table below)—represent God's design for all human relationships.

Healthy Human Relationships are:

Leave	Engaging
Cleave	Trusting
Weave	Productive

It is common for us to leave someone to be more present with others. As we attach ourselves to them, we build trust and we feel safe, and human society is generated. As already mentioned, mature adults, according to Erikson, express productivity through commitments to parenting, teaching, mentoring, civic activity, volunteer work—*as stakeholders and destiny shapers in society.* In society and, more specifically, the communities that we form, our lives are woven into new identities. We become known as

12. The Hebrew word for cleave is *davag.*

13. Eccl 4:8–12.

members of a family, inhabitants of a city or suburb, members of a church or club. Unfortunately, this blueprint for human life, according to the biblical narrative, took a nasty turn.

It Is a Story of De-Generativity

In Genesis 3 the story changes and human relationships become marked by *separation* and *disengagement*—words that remind me of apartheid and my response to James's request for affection. From that point onwards, the intimacy that existed between God and creation was disturbed by the intrusion of evil. The Biblical account is fascinating. Adam and Eve found themselves in a garden where there were two trees: the tree of life and the tree of the knowledge of good and evil. We do not really know what the second tree represents, but it seems that the trees symbolize the human freedom of choice. Satan exploited the human ability to choose, to achieve his own ends. Lasor et al describes it beautifully when he writes:

> The first sign of moral anarchy is declared through the serpent's obvious malevolent machinations. His subtle wiles induce the woman to doubt first God's word (3:1) and then God's goodness (vv 4f). Seeing the tree in an entirely different light (v.6), she takes its fruit and eats.[14]

I find it mind boggling that a seemingly simple act like this could have such far reaching effects. As the first humans ate from this tree they lost their intimacy with God and from this point all of humanity lost its innocence. Lasor describes it like this:

> In the sequel the altered relationship of humans with God is vividly pictured. The pair became ashamed of their nakedness (v.7; cf 2:25). Moreover, they flee in fear from the presence of God (v.8). The unity between the couple disintegrates. The new togetherness in sin does not unite but it divides. The man seeks to clear himself by placing guilt first on the woman and then on God (v.12). The woman, in turn, blames the serpent. Through proud ambition, Adam and Eve have become sinners and lost open fellowship with God. They must now wrestle with evil at all levels of their existence.[15]

14. Lasor et.al., *Old Testament Survey*, 26.
15. Ibid.

As I mentioned before, Aida Spenser describes the rest of life in the Old Testament as being under the curse, but it is clearly also a picture[16] of a situation that is getting steadily worse, that is de-generating. After the fall, we read in Genesis that God said to the serpent that his life would de-generate. He would live his life slithering on the ground and eating dust, nothing like the life he once had. The news was not any better for the first human couple. He said that Eve's body would de-generate and she would endure great pain in childbirth, and the earth in its de-generated state would cause Adam to toil to produce a crop. In addition, God decreed that they would need to leave Eden, and warned them that their relationship will also bear the marks of de-generation. God's *productive, generative, generous love* once marked their relationship, but now it will de-generate through power struggles. "You'll want to please your husband," God said to Eve, "but he'll lord it over you."[17]

Gilbert Bilezikian points us to the de-generative power of evil as he reflects on the Greek word for the personification of evil,[18] which as we mentioned before literally means "to throw across." He writes,

> A visual representation of oneness may be created instantly by clasping one's hands together. The hands are separate entities, each distinctively independent from the other. Yet the interlocked fingers of one's clasped hands suggest a bonding that makes them one body. After creating man and woman from one body, God declared them united into one flesh (Gen. 2:22–24). This joining together of two independent lives into oneness provides the basic model for biblical community.[19]

He goes on to say that the separation caused by evil can be illustrated by yanking apart the clutched hands. The consequence of this separation was far reaching. Bilezikian explains, "Unfortunately, the damage inflicted on oneness was far greater than mere separation. It led to ruler/subject hierarchy. This tragedy may be enacted with one hand made into a fist over the other."[20] Power struggles begin to dominate the storyline. We read about polygamy, slavery, murder, war, and children at risk. Human life is de-generating.

16. This is a term borrowed from Spencer, *Beyond the Curse*.
17. Gen 3:16 (The Message).
18. *Diabolos* can also be translated as "to pull apart or render asunder."
19. Bilezikian, *Community*, 45.
20. Ibid.

Opposite forces are at work. Instead of engagement, disengagement begins to mark human existence—an absent God, spouse, or parent. Instead of feeling safe with each other under God, humans fear the effects of distrust. The beauty of sexual intimacy that once pointed to the human ability to be productive is now the weapon in the war of the sexes. Evil turns presence into disengagement, trust into distrust, and instead of being productive, human life becomes unproductive—a sad picture of how something that was once beautiful steadily worsens.

3 Verbs	Generativity *Healthy Human Relationships are:*	De-generativity *Unhealthy Human Relationships are:*
Leave	Present	Dis-engaging
Cleave	Trusting	Dis-trusting
Weave	Productive	Unproductive

Life that is marked by disengagement, distrust, and de-generation is a hard life. It is a *hypo-reality.* In contrast to the Greek preposition *hyper*,[21] which means "over," *hypo*[22] means "beneath" or "less than." A world that is de-generating is a world that is a *hypo-reality*, a world that is under-par, *less than* what God intended it to be.

The way we deal with this *hypo-reality*, which we mentioned before, is to move in the opposite direction, we create a *hyper-reality.*[23] We act as if we have power to make it on our own, as if we have the power to stand alone. The easiest way to understand *hyper-reality* is to see it as a *hyped* or enhanced reality. In this reality the illusion of power becomes more important than the power itself. Baudrillard explains this by saying that power "produces nothing but signs of its resemblance."[24] In other words, it does not produce any true reality. And, says Jean Baudrillard, in this reality "there is no more hope for meaning."[25]

21. Greek: over; beyond; above, transcendental, exceeding, boundless, limitless and excessive, above normal.

22. Greek: under, below, beneath; less than; too little; deficient, diminished. Used as a prefix.

23. Greek: above, over; excessive; more than normal; abnormal excess [in medicine]; abnormally great or powerful sensation [in physical or pathological terms]; highest [in chemical compounds]. Used as a prefix.

24. Baudrillard, *Simulacra and Simulation*, 45.

25. Ibid., 164.

The 48 Laws of Power was a best seller in 2002. In the pocket-size version of this book, Robert Greene confirms Bilezikian's suspicions when he writes that "the feeling of not having power over people and events is generally unbearable to us—when we feel helpless we feel miserable. No one wants less power; everyone wants more."[26] This need for power may explain our current preoccupation with the power that we perceive leadership brings. It certainly serves as an illustration of the role of power in human relationships in a world that is in need of regeneration. The relationship between power and leadership is, after all, well established.[27] Harry Truman expressed this as follows: "Leadership is the ability to get men to do what they don't want to do and like it."[28]

A quick survey on the internet reveals how preoccupied we are with leadership. When I searched the web in 2004, Google delivered 21,500,000 articles on leadership in 0.17 seconds. In 2009, I found 125,000,000 in 0.24 seconds and in 2012, 503,000,000 in 0.08 seconds.[29] I wonder what it will be by the time you read these statistics.

Any respectable bookshop would reveal the general interest in leadership as well. In 2004, a librarian could stock his shelves with 85,665 books on leadership; five years later it was a bulging 372,859 volumes.[30] I think we are obsessed. In their book *Movies to Manage By*, John K. Clemens and Melora Wolff identify movies that are useful to develop a philosophy of leadership. *Apollo 13* teaches the importance of improvisation; *Dead Poets Society* speaks of the failed promise of heroic leadership; *Hoosiers* helps leaders turn their faltering team into a winning one; *Norma Rae* helps us to appreciate the value of mentoring and protégés; while *Citizen Kane* and *Wall Street* emphasize the importance of self-leadership. So, the examples continue. It is clear that leadership is a hot topic in Hollywood too.

While I believe that gifted leaders are a gift to society, I am nursing a hunch that our near obsession with leadership is our way of dealing with *hypo-reality*. Leadership today promises access to power, status, and money. I believe now that apartheid created a hyper-reality for white South

26. Greene, *48 Laws*, xi.

27. Gibson et al., *Organizations*, 333.

28. Cohen et al., *Effective Behavior*, 310.

29. Results achieved on ADSL in Australia. Type "Leadership" into Google.com search engine and see how many books are available today.

30. Type "Leadership" into the Amazon.com search engine and see how many books are available today.

Africans, and our unfettered access to power created the illusion that we are invincible.[31]

Leadership dominates the lecture circuit as well. Nelson Mandela (while he was able) and Bill Clinton are among those who are in high demand to share their experiences as leaders of nations facing challenges. Stacy Allison has been climbing mountains for the last twenty years. Now her experience as a mountaineer helps company executives take their companies to *new heights*. Like Stacy, other motivational speakers look for new and interesting angles to speak on this hot topic—Geese and Cheetahs are often on the agenda, or is that the menu? Even the *Khoisan* people, the so-called Bushmen of South Africa, do not escape the scrutiny of people who need new material for keynote addresses. It is the Bushmen's innate ability to focus on their prey, the way they find water in the desert, and their hunting prowess that are tantalizing traits too hard to ignore and too easy to exploit.

Leadership is a very popular topic in the church. Preachers point out that Aaron and Miriam struggled with Moses's popularity, while Moses himself grew weary under the pressure of leadership. They draw lessons from the leadership struggle between Saul, the first king of Israel, and his successor, David, who was the darling of the masses.

The church loves to reflect on David as a worthy model for leadership. He is, after all, a man after God's own heart. While I am in awe of David's relationship with God, I feel that preachers have to do scriptural gymnastics to make David's leadership a model for the twenty-first century. I wonder what David would have done if he was faced with the current problems in the Middle East. Given his weakness for beautiful women, would he perhaps have been the one explaining to the press what happened in the Oval Office? Would we find David searching the internet for x-rated sites while waiting for his men to return from battle in Iraq? The world of King David and the world today are like chalk and cheese, too far removed to make David a guru of leadership today.

David is also often used as justification for centralizing the leadership in one person in a local church—power by one over others. Thus, the church had a pope by the time of Constantine; a man of authority, the emperor of the church. The church had succumbed to the demands of civil society and, like the people of Israel, had chosen to place power in the hands of one

31. The current African National Congress Government of South Africa will also face this challenge today.

man. In parts of Christendom today there are other powerful men in positions of influence. Even in the newer expressions of Christianity, such as the Pentecostal, Charismatic, and Apostolic movements, power is often vested in one person. The monarch seems to be alive and well in the church today.

This obsession with leadership is something that even the disciples of Jesus struggled with. In an intimate moment, the mother of two brother-disciples of Jesus approached him with a burning request. "Grant that one of these two sons of mine may sit at your right and the other at your left in your kingdom,"[32] she asked. The kingdom was about to be revealed, the masses were about to be ruled by a new king, and he would need lieutenants.

Jesus's response has been a pet scripture of pastors through the ages as they have preached on the topic of servant leadership. He said, "Whoever wants to become great among you must be your servant, and whoever wants to be first must be your slave—just as the Son of Man did not come to be served, but to serve, and to give his life as a ransom for many."[33] The motivation of this response is, however, often ignored. Jesus said that Gentile rulers "lord it over"[34] those that they are supposed to lead; something Jesus despised.

Our obsession with leadership (or rather, with what we feel leadership will give us) is one way in which power seems to be the default position we return to when we feel anxious. We counter anxiety by grabbing power to assert ourselves over others. As we have seen, for Paul Tillich and Ted Peters, this anxiety results from our separation from the *ground of our being*. A more faithful response to *hypo-reality* and its concomitant anxiety would be to not take matters into our own hands in an attempt to escape pain in this world, but rather to discover ourselves in the narrative of God and in the midst of the hard realities of life.

The unfolding story of Scripture suggests that God's love can break into our anxiety-ridden existence. God climbs onto a cross and puts his existence at risk not so that we escape *hypo-reality*, but that we learn to live faithfully in it. This points us to the third movement of the Christian story—regeneration—which we will explore more fully in the next section of this chapter. In another passage, Paul explains that God destroyed the effects of *evil* through the events of Easter. In *The Message*, Eugene Peterson translates it like this:

32. Matt 20:21 (NIV).

33. Ibid. 20:26–27.

34. Ibid. 20:25.

> The Messiah has made things up between us so that we're now together on this, both non-Jewish outsiders and Jewish insiders. He tore down the wall we used to keep each other at a distance. He repealed the law code that had become so clogged with fine print and footnotes that it hindered more than it helped. Then he started over. Instead of continuing with two groups of people separated by centuries of animosity and suspicion, he created a new kind of human being, a fresh start for everybody. Christ brought us together through his death on the cross. The cross got us to embrace, and that was the end of the hostility. Christ came and preached peace to you outsiders and peace to us insiders. He treated us as equals, and so made us equals. Through him we both share the same Spirit and have equal access to the Father.[35]

This is what I experienced after my encounter with James. At seminary I was able to process this new reality. God had entered my world through James and Marian, and I knew that we would need to return to South Africa to be part of God's plan to bring reconciliation between the race groups of South Africa.

This envisioned unity was far from the minds of most South African in 1985 when Marian and I returned to South Africa. Marian, who had begun to process the changes that were taking place in me, and I returned to a South Africa that was literally burning with rage and racial hatred. We arrived back in South Africa a few months after one of the most destructive car bombs exploded in Pretoria, the city where I received my first pastoral appointment. Here is how the BBC reported on that tragic day:

> At least 16 people have been killed and more than 130 people injured in a car bomb explosion in South Africa's capital city, Pretoria. The explosion happened outside the Nedbank Square building on Church Street at about 16:30 hours—the height of the city's rush hour. More than 20 ambulances attended the scene and took the dead and injured to three hospitals in and around Pretoria. Police sealed off the surrounding area with a barbed-wire fence as emergency personnel sifted through the rubble looking for bodies. Bomb disposal experts were called to the scene to search for

35. Eph 2:14–18 (The Message). The NIV translates it like this: "For he himself is our peace, who has made the two one and has destroyed the barrier, the dividing wall of hostility, by abolishing in his flesh the law with its commandments and regulations. His purpose was to create in himself one new man out of the two, thus making peace, and in this one body to reconcile both of them to God through the cross, by which he put to death their hostility. He came and preached peace to you who were far away and peace to those who were near. For through him we both have access to the Father by one Spirit."

> a possible second bomb. The outlawed anti-apartheid group the African National Congress has been blamed for the attack.[36]

This report is in a stark contrast with the vision that Paul had for life beyond the cross. As a young, white, Afrikaner couple in our mid-twenties, we knew that we would have to make some hard decisions in the months following our return. What had happened to me in Atlanta would be tested. We understood that what was happening in South Africa represented a life that was in need of regeneration.

It Is a Story of Regeneration

We are following the story that has given direction to my life. As we have seen it starts with the garden in which Adam and Eve live generatively as adults. They are shaping a world in which their children would find a future with God and his creation. But sadly, as we discussed in the previous section, it is also a story of stagnation, one in which humans succumb to the de-generative forces in the world. The story, fortunately, has a third act, one that is unfolding as I write these words. It is a story that involves and affects all of us today. It is a story that unfolds after the cross and resurrection of Christ.

Living a regenerative life is perilous yet vocational living, because it takes place between the *already* and the *not yet* in God's story (see diagram below). This is also known as Inaugural Eschatology,[37] which argues that the Kingdom of God has broken in human reality and that this Kingdom is advancing against the influence of Satan in this world. And while the ultimate victory is not yet evident, it will be evident when Christ returns. The *already/not yet* distinction has long been employed as short-hand for: the Kingdom of God is already present but not yet complete. It is not only true that our lives are being regenerated as a result of what happened at Easter; it is also true that our lives are becoming vehicles of Easter—lives that resist entropy and stagnation. We all therefore live in the so-called tension between the already and the not yet. Liminality as Victor Turner

36. http://news.bbc.co.uk/onthisday/hi/dates/stories/may/20/newsid_4326000/4326975.stm, accessed May 9, 2010.

37. Eschatology is a theological study of the end-times. It has particular interest in the second coming of Christ. Students of Geerhardus Vos and Herman Ridderbos and George Eldon Ladd have promoted this idea for decades already. I was introduced to it in the late 1970s as part of my pre-theology course at university.

describes it is, I think, a great description for the in-between space that we find ourselves in after Easter. He once said that liminality is an in-between state, it is a threshold experience and, while we are in the liminal state:

> Human beings are stripped of anything that might differentiate them from their fellow human beings—they are in between the social structure, temporarily fallen through the cracks, so to speak, and it is in these cracks, in the interstices of social structure, that they are most aware of themselves. Yet liminality is a midpoint between a starting point and an ending point, and as such it is a temporary state that ends when the initiate is reincorporated into the social structure.[38]

It is a bit like driving in a heavy rainstorm: if you stop you might put other lives in danger, but to go forward may be just as perilous since all you have to go by are the faint road markings that come and go under the searching lights of your car. Yet, you know that there is really only one way, and that is forward.

In the tension between the already and the not yet, we are aware of the unfaith that is still in us; the desire to take matters into our own hands. At the same time we have the effects of Easter already at work within us; *our lives are hidden in Christ with God*; we are being regenerated.

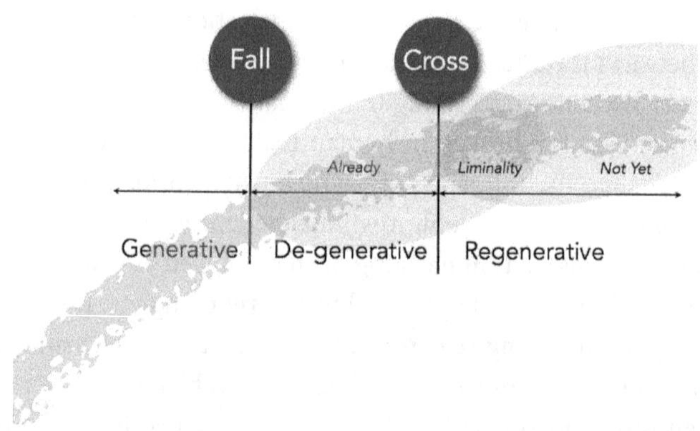

What makes it difficult is that we need to discover our own way through this liminal space. The storyline of Scripture curves towards freedom in Christ,[39] and we need to find a way that resists the slavery, racism, and

38. La Shure, "What is Liminality?" accessed June 11, 2012, http://www.liminality.org/about/whatisliminality.

39. See Gal 4:8–11.

sexism of our former de-generative way of living. Jolande Jacobi a Jungian analyst in her famous book, *The Way of Individuation* (1965), describes the psychological process that is involved in finding your own way as "following [A] labyrinthine winding." From birth to death, she says, we try to find our own way. Most of this is done "unreflectively, unconsciously and even unsuspectingly," but even so, we are motivated by hope and longing. She warns that this is not for the faint-hearted. Only if we tread the path bravely and fling ourselves into life, "fearing no struggle and no exertion and fighting shy of no experience, will we mature our personality more fully than the person who is ever trying to keep to the safe side of the road."[40]

When we first went to the United States of America I had a safe plan for the rest of my life. My plan was to complete the Master's degree, return to South Africa, and then complete further qualifications in psychology. I believed these qualifications would give me a career as a psychologist or a pastor and, if this failed, I would become an academic. I had a strategy and a story to live by—albeit a very thin story, an easy way through. But the story of my life took a different turn after my encounter with James, and after I emerged from Pitts Theological Library in Atlanta. I sensed there was a new longing and desire, one that I was unfamiliar with. I knew that the prejudices that marked my life before James could no longer be part the story that would shape my world.

The analogy of the searching lights of a car in the rain that we used is helpful to a point, but perhaps it breaks down when it suggests that we are out in the rain alone. The reality is that, while we are searching for the storyline in the tension between the already and the not yet, God is calling us. Faith trusts the voice of God; it seeks and responds to the voice of God in the midst of many voices. Frederick Buechner says that there are many voices that want to guide us through the *labyrinthine winding*, it could be society, the superego, self-interest, but it could be God. There is a way, he says, to tell if it is God's voice. "The kind of work God usually calls you to do is work (a) that you need most to do and (b) that the world needs most to have done. The place God calls you to is the place where your deep gladness and the world's deep hunger meet."[41]

40. Jacobi, *Way of Individuation*, 16–17. I have changed the personal pronouns to be more gender-inclusive.

41. Buechner, *Wishful Thinking*, 95.

A regenerative life is vocational,[42] and this kind of life is beautifully revealed in Jesus of the Gospels. There is probably no better example of someone discerning the different voices that were coming at him than the one we have in Jesus's encounter with the tempter in the desert. For some, this story is about how we overcome temptation in our lives, but it seems to many others and myself, that there is more at stake here. The temptation of Jesus has become a model for me of how we find our way in this liminal space, this in-between space of the already and the not yet. This story became my compass as Marian and I returned to South Africa with a desire to help bring reconciliation in South Africa. It is to this story that we now turn.

42. *Vocare* is a form of a Latin word meaning "to call."

7

Hero Minding

Following Jesus in Liminality

With a renewed faith in God and the growing understanding of the Story that we find ourselves in we returned to South Africa. I was ordained in the denomination of my childhood, but within a year I received orders to join the South African Defence Force to complete my compulsory military service. It quickly became evident to me that it would be a challenge to reconcile a denominational career with my sense of God's call to do my part in resisting the evil effects of apartheid. The denomination I was part of required I comply with the orders of the state, but I knew my commitment to social-justice would not allow me to take up arms. Because I was already married and I was facing a prison sentence if I refused to serve in the military, I chose the lesser of two evils; I would serve my time as a non-combatant. But I was deeply unhappy.

This time in my life highlighted the tension of liminality. Paul the Apostle says it well: "It happens so regularly that it's predictable. The moment I decide to do good, sin is there to trip me up. I truly delight in God's commands, but it's pretty obvious that not all of me joins in that delight. Parts of me covertly rebels, and just when I least expect it, they take charge."[1] How do we find we live in this liminal space between the already and the not yet of the Kingdom of God that Jesus came to establish here on earth? This was and still is the sacred question.

1. Rom 7:21–23 (The Message).

I soon discovered that the story of Jesus's temptation provides very important signposts as we traverse liminality. Jesus is in a liminal space in the desert and he finds a way through. In the chronology of the Gospels, Jesus is *full of the Holy Ghost* and was *led by the Spirit into the wilderness*[2] from the Jordan River. At the Jordan River he heard that his father was pleased with him, and he experienced the presence of the Holy Spirit. It would have been an exhilarating experience, one that would have filled Jesus with great joy and hope. But now, still full of the Holy Spirit, Jesus is led into the desert.

I find it is interesting that Jesus, after the forty days in the desert, is described as being *in the power of the Spirit.*[3] Is this different to being *full of the Holy Spirit* before the temptation? And now, Jesus immediately goes into a nearby synagogue and he chooses a text that would define his vocation. As I mentioned before, for some, this story is about how we overcome temptation in our lives, but that it seems to many others and myself that there is more at stake here. The temptation of Jesus has become a model for me of how we find our way in this liminal space. I need to mind this story as I find my way through the liminality of being between the already and the not yet.

Jesus Was Engaged

We note, firstly, that Jesus refused to turn stones into bread. On the face of it, this does not seem to be a great temptation. It is not as if Satan was tempting Jesus to turn methamphetamine crystals into *ice.*[4] No, it was simply to turn stones into bread. What was the big deal?

Jesus, however, seemed to be alert to the fact that Satan wanted him to take care of his own immediate needs—to take matters into his own hands. For Jesus, there was clearly more at stake and his hunger could wait. What he needed more were the words that are like bread, which would come from his Father's mouth.

2. Luke 4:1 (NIV).

3. Luke 4:14.

4. See http://www.druginfo.adf.org.au/fact-sheets/ice-crystal-methamphetamine-hydrochloride. "Ice" is a street name for crystal methamphetamine hydrochloride, which is a powerful, synthetic stimulant drug. Stimulant drugs speed up the messages going to and from the brain. Ice is more potent than other forms of amphetamines. It is more pure than the powder form of methamphetamine ("speed").

This is an unusual picture that Jesus references; one that is taken from the world of birds. Little chicks in a nest have their mouths filled with the food that literally comes from their mother's mouth. Without this food the young ones will die. In the same way, without the words that come from God's mouth, Jesus was hopeless. He needed to hear his Father's voice and be in his presence. The human equivalent for this would be milk from a mother's breast—an image we can comfortably apply to God.

The earliest picture of God as a *mother* is in the story of creation. The Hebrew word *to brood over*[5] can also be translated as: *to hover with a gentle fluttering motion*. Herman Schultz, in an Old Testament classic, picks up on the bird-like actions of the Spirit when he writes, "Over the lifeless and formless mass of the world-matter this Spirit broods like a bird on its nest, and thus transmits to it the seeds of life, so that afterwards by the word of God it can produce whatever God wills."[6] This is a beautiful picture of a maternal God who brings life to her creation. Here God gives birth to the universe. One of the first things we know about God is that he is present in his creation and that he speaks as he creates.

God could instruct humans in Genesis 2 that relationships are established through being present, by leaving and cleaving to another, because that is what he did. When God said, "Let us create," there was no time outside of God, there was only God. Theology teaches us that the first thing that God created in his act of creation was space itself. It is as if God *experienced* a kind of leaving at this point. Moltmann explains that "he therefore goes creatively 'out of himself,' communicating himself to the one who is other than himself."[7] There was a time when there was only God, but then God made space within himself to have relationships with beings that were created by him. Moltmann is once again very helpful when he says: "In order to create something outside himself, the infinite God must have made room for this finitude beforehand, 'in himself.'"[8] And in this time and space, God brooded like a bird on a nest.

It seems that God is passionate about creating space for life; creating space for creatures to know his presence, to hear his voice and to live in the space that God has created, to engage him. Like little chicks in a nest have their mouths filled by the food that comes from their mother's mouth, we

5. Hebrew word, *rahapl.*

6. Schultz, *Old Testament Theology*, 184.

7. Moltmann, *Trinity*, 117ff.

8. Ibid.

were designed for intimacy with God; to live in the spaciousness of the mutual indwelling that the church fathers described, and to hear his voice.

The Garden of Eden is the space that God made for humans to be present for others in creation but also, perhaps most of all, to know his presence. When I think about God and what he is passionate about, one of the first things that come to my mind is that he makes space for people to know his life-giving presence. God makes space for life, space in which we can engage him.

We need to have a deeper understanding of presence, so I will need to take you into the world of Hebrew and Greek yet again. In the Hebrew Bible, *kabod* is the word for God's presence. It refers to the light that beamed down onto the Ark of the Covenant. It would be the right word to capture Adam and Eve's experience of God's presence in the garden. Later, *kabod* was translated as *doxa* in Greek Old Testament, and then as "glory" in the English Bible. *Doxa*, as the beam of God's light on the tabernacle, was more than just a show—it was a tangible demonstration of God's presence; God indwelling space and time. God's glory is his presence. When humans hear him, they are normally overwhelmed and fall down under the weight of his voice.

In the desert, Jesus is reminded that he could satisfy his physical hunger with bread made from stones, but Jesus sees through this. He prefers to live by every word that comes from his Father's mouth. He prefers the *doxa* of God. Did God as Spirit not lead him into the desert? Was he not called to this place? Or, as Buechner pointed out, is this not the most urgent work that Jesus had to do and that the world needs most to have done? Was the desert not his Garden of Eden where he would be in the presence of his Father through the Spirit?

To succumb to Satan would mean that he withdraws, that he disengages himself from God, that he ignores words that could feed him, call him. This would be heterodoxy rather than orthodoxy! Orthodoxy[9] is to stay in God's presence; it is to engage God as we listen for his voice. This is why over the years, *orthodoxy* has come to mean right belief, or the correct handling of the Word. For years I believed that someone is *orthodox* in his or her faith if they commit to what is the true, exact, and intact teaching of Christ is in all its purity and fullness, as if that is entirely possible.

9. *Orthos* speaks of something that is "straight" or "right." *Doxa* means "glory" or "worship."

3 Verbs	Generativity *Healthy Human Relationships are:*	Jesus in liminality	Our way through liminality
Leave	Present	Engaged his Father	Orthodoxy: engage God as we listen for his voice.

While correct doctrine should be our aim, it somehow seems to fall short if God's voice cannot be heard above the clutter of other voices and the noises in our own thinking. If we do not live as if these truths are like bread to our bodies, then we have disengaged and we could just as well satisfy our growling stomachs. There is little doubt in my mind that the beginning point of theology is to be engaged with God and to choose God's voice above anything or anyone else. This does not mean that we retreat to a monastery, as much as that might be an option at times, but rather it is to engage God in this time and space, in everyday life, in the liminal space between the already and not yet. Jesus would rather stay hungry in God's presence, to hear his voice, than to satisfy his hunger and be disengaged.

To live a regenerative life in the tension between the already and not yet is fraught with danger. Jesus was in that space; it was a threshold experience for him. In this place he makes a decision that will help all of us; he chooses one voice to listen to and to remain engaged. What does this mean for us as we face our own liminality? N. T. Wright gives the answer when he writes, "It is a central part of the Christian vocation to learn to recognize the voices that whisper attractive lies, to distinguish them from the voice of God, and to use the simple but direct weapons provided in Scripture to rebut the lies with truth."[10]

We discover the regenerative storyline when we develop a greater dependence on God's voice through the study of Scripture and doctrine, listening to the testimonies of others and learning our own experiences. As Jesus listened to every word that proceeded from his Father's mouth, the one who said that he could not live on bread alone became the Bread of Life. As the voice of the Father became clearer, so too did the vocation of Jesus. One could say that Jesus as a man had a growing knowledge of his vocation. Wright explains that, Jesus's knowledge of his vocation was more risky, it was not as certain as knowing that one is hungry or not. It was a more significant knowing; "*like knowing one is loved. One cannot 'prove' it*

10. Wright, *Luke*, 44.

except by living by it."[11] His vocation emerged as he discerned the voice of his Father, as he took bread from his Father's mouth. Wright sums it up well when he says,

> Jesus of Nazareth was conscious of a vocation: a vocation, given him by the one he knew as "father," to enact in himself what, in Israel's scriptures, God had promised to accomplish all by himself. He would be the pillar of cloud and fire for the people of the new exodus. He would embody in himself the returning and redeeming action of the covenant God.[12]

This has huge implications for those who are followers of Jesus. As we live in the tension between the already and the not yet we need to not only listen for the voice of God, but we have to trust his work and purposes. The image of the potter often comes to my mind when I think about this. The Bible loves this image and so do I. God is described as the potter, and his people as the clay in his hands. Sometimes the clay is removed from the potter's wheel to enable the potter to remove the air-bubbles from the clay. These are often very dark times for the person who has this *off-the-wheel* experience. Peterson's description of this is poetically beautiful and hilarious: "You made me like a handcrafted piece of pottery—and now are you going to smash me to pieces? Don't you remember how beautifully you worked my clay? Will you reduce me now to a mud pie?"[13]

The message of faith in the story of the potter and the clay is that even while the clay is off the potter's wheel, it is still in the potter's hands. The potter is creating a masterpiece, a work of art that has purpose and value.[14] In his letter to the followers of Jesus in Ephesus, Paul says that the masterpiece that is being formed on the potter's wheel is a regenerative life that is vocational. He writes: "He creates each of us by Christ Jesus to join him in the work he does, the good work he has gotten ready for us to do, work we had better be doing."[15] Orthodoxy is to stay in God's presence; it is to engage God as we listen for his voice.

This early signpost in Jesus's story brought us to the realization that we would have to make life-altering decisions shortly after our return to

11. Wright, *Jesus*, 653.

12. Wright, *Luke*, 44.

13. Job 10:8–9 (The Message).

14. See the NIV translation of Ephesians 2:10, "For we are God's workmanship, created in Christ Jesus to do good works, which God prepared in advance for us to do."

15. Ibid.

South Africa in 1985. I could not serve two masters: career and vocation. I realized that I would remain conflicted as long as I was pursuing a career that was detached from my vocation. As soon as I could, after military service, Marian and I accepted a call to become the director of a small Bible Institute in Cape Town.

Here, Marian and I became part of a community that was being victimized by apartheid. We left our extended family in Johannesburg to be present in a new place with a new community. We changed our home language from Afrikaans to English as an act of protest, and I became an ordained minister in the *colored* department of the church. While this was all very significant, I was only satisfied that I had finally responded to the call of God when I became a conscientious objector, but more about this later.

Jesus Worshipped

As we pick up again on the story in the desert, we see Jesus's tempter offer him all the kingdoms of the world; all Jesus had to do was bow down and worship him. This seems more serious than turning stones into bread. Satan is proposing a new alliance of sorts. He wants Jesus to cleave to him and to let go of his relationship with his Father through the Spirit. If Jesus bows the knee before Satan he will receive as his reward, power and authority over the kingdoms of the world. The link between worship and reward is a well-established link in religion.[16] Some worshippers might believe that if they worship in a certain way (e.g., bring their offerings) that the god or gods would reward them for being good. This is what Satan proposes: "Jesus worship me, and I will reward you by giving you all the kingdoms of the earth."

This idea, *to worship for a reward*, is still prevalent in modern-day Christianity. James Torance writes,

> We go to church, we sing our psalm and hymns to God, we intercede for the world, we listen to the sermon (too often simply an exhortation), we offer our money, time and talents to God. No doubt we need God's grace to do it. We do it because Jesus taught us to do it and left us an example of how to do it. But worship is what we do before God . . . We sit in the pew watching the minister "doing his thing," exhorting us "to do our thing" until we go home thinking we have done our duty for another week! This kind of

16. *Latreuo* in its most basic sense means "to serve for hire."

> "do it yourself with the help of the minister" worship is what our forefathers would have called "legal worship" and not "evangelical worship."[17]

That was certainly true for me for most of my childhood. Worship was linked to reward; God has saved me and so I do something for God in return, then God will do something for me, and so on. This was Satan's view of worship too, he makes Jesus an offer that is better than the offer that is on the proverbial table and thinks that Jesus is bound to come his way.

How infinitely richer is Jesus's understanding of worship though: an understanding that is not based on economic rationalities, but one that flows from his deep love and intimate union with his Father. This union is the subject of the Gospels, and Torrance is right when he says,

> At the center of the New Testament stands not our religious experience, not our faith or repentance or decision, however important these are, but a unique relationship . . . between Jesus and the Father. Christ is presented to us as the Son living a life of union and communion with the Father in the Spirit, presenting himself in our humanity through the eternal Spirit to the Father on behalf of humankind.[18]

For Jesus to worship Satan would mean that he would need to sacrifice his union with the Father and Spirit. This simply would not happen, for there is no deeper expression of cleaving in the universe than in the Trinity—the Son living a life of union and communion with the Father in the Spirit. I do not know how well Jesus understood this in his humanness. It is not clear whether Jesus had a fully developed sense of his ontological union with the Father through the Spirit as he faced his tormentor. What we do know is that this temptation was real and that Jesus had a real choice—to choose to cleave to his Father, to trust him, or to accept Satan's offer.

This insight introduces another very important issue for those who live in liminality like us. In this in-between place of liminality, it is a real temptation to put our trust in status, power, and money. In this hyped-reality of status, power, and money, the pain of hypo-reality begins to fade and as our love for the *kingdoms of this world* take hold of us, we begin to lose sight of who we are—image bearers of God.

17. Torrance, *Worship*, 20.

18. Ibid., 30–31.

The choice is very clear for Jesus, he can choose to remain true to who he is—the one who had just heard at the Jordan River that he is "God's beloved Son"—or he can switch allegiance and receive all the kingdoms on offer. In the desert the question is not only *who* am I, it is also, *whose* am I? Jesus, however, had somehow internalized the truth spoken at the River Jordan. If we can understand why Jesus decided to reject Satan's offer, we will also find insight into how we can deal with hyper-reality in our own liminality.

Jesus, as we have seen, had to recognize the voice of the Father among many other voices, but now he had to internalize the voice of God. This is a vital lesson for all of us who live in liminality. This insight is beautifully illustrated by one of my favorite Old Testament stories. The people of Israel are in the desert on their way to the Promised Land. God is kind to his people, and he demonstrates his nearness by giving them cloud cover by day and a column of fire by night. Interestingly, God's presence is often demonstrated in the Old Testament by clouds.[19] It is very likely that the Jews experienced the cloud as God's face over them because the word for "face" and "presence" are very similar in the Hebrew.[20]

Consider, though, the story of when the twelve spies are sent off to explore the land that God is giving them. We are told that the cloud did not go with them. They are now in the same position that Jesus was in during his temptation. Most of us know the rest of this story: ten of the spies return totally overwhelmed by what they saw and experienced. According to these men, the task of taking the land is too great and it would be better to abandon the mission. The two remaining spies respond differently, saying: "If the Lord is pleased with us, he will lead us into that land, a land flowing with milk and honey, and will give it to us."[21] The difference between the two and the ten is that the former had developed *presence permanence*, a form of object permanence.

We know from developmental psychology that in the early stages of development children believe that if objects are no longer visible to them, they do not exist. Object permanence is when toddlers realize that out of sight does not mean out of existence. I remember when Zoé, our youngest daughter, as a toddler, lost a coin that her grandfather gave her. She cried out: "Get it. Get it," as I watched it roll into a storm water drain. "Don't

19. See Ex 16:10; 40:34–35; Num 11:25; 12:5.

20. Seow, "Face," 323.

21. Num 14:8 (NIV).

worry," I glibly responded, "I will give you another one. It does not matter." But she was inconsolable, "It won't be that one; it matters to me," she cried. She had developed object permanence.

Caleb and Joshua demonstrated object permanence as well. We read that God says of the two spies that they followed him *wholeheartedly*—they were able to remain in God's presence even when the cloud was not visible. They remained aware of his presence and so they were able to be passionate about what he was passionate about. They wanted to inherit the promise that God made to their people.

Jesus internalized the voice he heard while he was being baptized, and that would shape his affections deeply and profoundly for the rest of his life. While he was facing the choice between being given all the earthly kingdoms on a platter versus a growing awareness that his life is special, he could hear the voice say, "This is my beloved Son, in him I am well pleased." Eugene Petersen says Jesus's refusal of Satan's offer was curt: "Beat it, Satan!" he said. He backed his rebuke with a third quotation from Deuteronomy: "Worship the Lord your God, and only him. Serve him with absolute single-heartedness."[22] This is *orthopathy* it means to trust God as we internalize his voice of passion for us. This too, is what we need as we face our own liminality.

3 Verbs	Generativity *Healthy human relationships are:*	Jesus in liminality	Our way through liminality
Leave	Present	Engaged his Father	Orthodoxy: engage God as we listen for his voice
Cleave	Trusting	Jesus Worshipped	Orthopathy: to trust God as we internalize his voice of passion for us

Who and what do we worship? Whose voice do we trust most? Whose passion do we respond to? Who are our closest allies? These are some of the most basic questions we need to answer in this liminal space. In this space we need to internalize God's voice of affection in our lives. This is why Torrance's description of worship rings true for me. In worship God "lifts

22. Matt 4:10 (The Message).

us up out of ourselves to participate in the very life and communion of the Godhead, that life of communion for which we were created."[23]

In worship, we are reminded that our lives are special and that it is folded into the life of God. It would be therefore a mistake to think of worship as only the event that occurs on a Sunday during mass, communion, or the church service. It is that, but it is much more; it is to live with a profound sense of a life wrapped in the life of God—of cleaving. It is to live with a sense of God's deep affection for us and our affection for God in return. Ultimately, it is to trust that God is good and that we can live our lives, as ordinary human beings, with his voice deeply internalized in our being.

Jesus Stayed True to His Calling

After Jesus refused to turn stones into bread he was tempted to jump from the top of the temple.[24] As many other commentators have suggested, I am sure that Jesus would have loved to bypass all the suffering, ignore the difficulty that would come from being a vocational Messiah, and miss the cross altogether. Taking shortcuts is a very real temptation in liminal spaces.

Jumping from the top of the temple seems to be good career advice if Jesus wants a shortcut to advance his career as a Messiah. As his accuser pointed out, if he was the Messiah, then surely Psalm 91 would be fulfilled and God would place him *in the care of angels*. This would be an incredible media stunt; Jesus would land perfectly on the doorstep of the temple in plain sight of all the religious leaders. There would be no doubt that he was a serious contender to be the Messiah of whom the Old Testament scriptures speak. This was not a bad option if Jesus was going to take matters into his own hands to advance his career. If Jesus wanted a career path that led to fame, then why not take the shortest possible route to that point? While this would advance Jesus's career as a Messiah, it would not shape the destiny of generation to come; it would not be generative. And so Jesus says to his tempter, "Don't you dare test the Lord your God."

23. Torrance, *Worship*, 22.

24. See how The Message translates Matthew 4:5–7: "For the second test the Devil took him to the Holy City. He sat him on top of the Temple and said, "Since you are God's Son, jump." The Devil goaded him by quoting Psalm 91: "He has placed you in the care of angels. They will catch you so that you won't so much as stub your toe on a stone." Jesus countered with another citation from Deuteronomy: "Don't you dare test the Lord your God."

This sounds very similar to what we see when Jesus announced to his disciples nearly three years later, that he would choose to die in order to follow the voice of God. His disciples could not understand this. Only a few minutes before that, they had come to the jubilant realization that he was the "the Christ, the Messiah." Messiahs do not die. In their minds, if Jesus was truly the Messiah, then he would gather an army to break the yoke of foreign oppression and restore the temple to its original glory—surely he would not offer himself as a sacrifice. The insistence by Peter that this should not happen draws a sharp reaction from Jesus: "Peter, get out of my way! Satan, get lost! You have no idea how God works."[25]

This was such a vulnerable moment in the desert. Jesus could choose the way of the career Messiah or he could demonstrate the characteristics of a vocational Messiah. The latter is far more difficult than the former but, because he chose to follow God's voice, the New Testament tells the story of a different kind of Messiah. One who was able to liberate Israel from a deeper oppression than the oppression that was caused by Rome. One who, instead of re-establishing Jerusalem as the religious capital of the world, was able to send his followers from Jerusalem to the uttermost parts of the world. Instead of rebuilding the temple, he was able to create a temple that is not made of brick and mortar, but rather one made of human beings who individually and collectively become temples through the Holy Spirit.

If I was a movie director and I was to make a movie of this moment in the temptation, I would be inclined to create a scene where the Tempter appears in the guise of a football scout to Jesus and his Father. Jesus and his Father have been discussing the family business and Jesus's future role in it, but the scout puts up a strong case. He describes a future away from the drudgery of the family business, away from the long hours and the boring routines. Jesus can walk away right there, take his future in his own hands and be *free*, but his Father refuses and Jesus stays.

This would not be an accurate representation of the story as it unfolds in the gospels though. What is remarkable about this story is that there is

25. See The Message: He then asked, "And you—what are you saying about me? Who am I?" Peter gave the answer: "You are the Christ, the Messiah." Jesus warned them to keep it quiet, not to breathe a word of it to anyone. He then began explaining things to them: "It is necessary that the Son of Man proceed to an ordeal of suffering, be tried and found guilty by the elders, high priests, and religion scholars, be killed, and after three days rise up alive." He said this simply and clearly so they couldn't miss it. But Peter grabbed him in protest. Turning and seeing his disciples wavering, wondering what to believe, Jesus confronted Peter. "Peter, get out of my way! Satan, get lost! You have no idea how God works."

no evidence of God the Father's interference with the decision that Jesus is about to make. We do not read: "and a voice thundered from heaven and said, 'Watch out my son, this is a trap.'" Apart from reading that Jesus was led into the desert to be tempted, the involvement of God as Father is never mentioned again. And yet his voice is heard.

Jesus refused to take the shortcut to personal glory and fame because he knew how to discern the voice of his Father among many voices and because he trusted that voice above any other. He stays in his Father's business. He shared God's passion to see creation restored to its original state. Jesus's passion was not for fame; it was to see creation liberated and redeemed. Jesus is a stakeholder in creation, his calling in life is to shape this world to be in union with God again. He is being adult.

It does not escape me that in Christian tradition Jesus is the *Logos*—the Word of God. He was the one through whom all things were created. Peterson translates it like this:

> The Word was first, the Word present to God, God present to the Word. The Word was God, in readiness for God from day one. Everything was created through him; nothing—not one thing!—came into being without him. What came into existence was Life, and the Life was Light to live by. The Life-Light blazed out of the darkness; the darkness couldn't put it out.[26]

I do not know if Jesus, in his humanness, had a full understanding of this. If he did, it raises question about just how human he was. What we do know as onlookers and participants in this unfolding drama is that Jesus was instrumental in creation and through him creation comes to its full potential. Jesus created the very kingdoms of the earth, and much more than the earth, all of creation. The universe proceeded from Jesus, and it came about through an intimate relationship between the Father, Son, and Holy Spirit. All things were created in partnership with God the Father and through the Spirit. As we saw in the previous section, he did not create so that he could receive his Father's affirmation or some heavenly reward. No, he created because that was the thing he was called to do. That was what God wanted him to do; it was where his deep gladness to serve and the Trinity's passion to create met. It was his vocation.

We noted earlier how quickly the harmony and peace in the Garden of Eden had been disturbed after the fall. In the stifling atmosphere of one-upmanship, Adam lorded it over his wife and creation, Eve cried in pain

26. John 1:1–5 (The Message).

as her first son was born and again when his brother took his life. Life had become stagnant and polluted.

"Fatedness" is James Fowler's choice term to describe the nature of human existence after the fall. Fatedness suggests that sin has placed human life on a predetermined path that takes us away from the freedom that God intended for us. "In fatedness, destinies and futures become congealed in destructive forms that are in enmity against God's future," says Fowler.[27] In a way, fatedness becomes a colonizing power that drains creation of all its spiritual vitality and leaves humans with death as the inevitable conclusion of life. In Jesus, however, God enters our stagnant pools of "subverted destiny and freedom"[28] and in the Christ act, God makes himself known as the liberator and redeemer.

Satan wants Jesus to forget his vocation and to follow a career that will lead to his own fame and fortune, but Jesus resists that temptation, as he would again three years later when the disciples want to stop him from dying in Jerusalem. But being generative meant that Jesus would also do the right thing—*orthopraxy.*[29] Jesus will stay true to his calling, to see the creation that he helped to create become free and fulfilled once again. If sin is, as Fowler defines it, "the tendency of creatures, acting in destiny and freedom, to veer away from God's intended future,"[30] then Jesus is passionate about seeing creation return to God's intended future. This is his vocation, his calling.

For most of my life, I saw orthopraxy as the *right practices* that we do to earn brownie points with God. I thought that my right practices could somehow neutralize all the bad things that I might get up to on an ordinary day. It is strange now to reflect on how egocentric so much of my theology has been.

There is much more than this to *orthopraxy*. I think that the "right" in *right practice* refers to more than doing good. This is *orthopraxy*—it means that as image bearers of God, we embrace our vocation to join God in his good intention for creation. James Fowler explains his understanding of God's good intentions like this: "Our effort to elaborate the outline of a theology of God's creative work led us to see that there is purposefulness and intentional structure built into the space, time and matter that came

27. Fowler, *Faith Development*, 43.

28. Ibid., 44.

29. Praxis is combined with the Greek word *orthos* to speak of right practices.

30. Fowler, *Faith Development*, 43.

into being in creation."[31] Christ is the Word through whom all creation came about and he is the purpose that is built into the heart of creation.[32] As humans we have acted, and we continue to act, contrary to God's righteous intentions for creation. When we do so, we lose our freedom. If a locomotive becomes unhappy with the lack of freedom that it needs to endure on the confines of the steel track, it need only wonder what it would be to not have the tracks at all. It seems quite reasonable to say that we are most free when we live according to God's intention for human life.

3 Verbs	Generativity *Healthy Human Relationships are:*	Jesus in liminality	Our way through liminality
Leave	Present	Engaged his Father	Orthodoxy: engage God as we listen for his voice
Cleave	Trusting	Jesus Worshipped	Orthopathy: to trust God as we internalise his voice of passion for us
Weave	Productive	Jesus stayed true to his calling	*Orthopraxy*: that as image bearers of God we embrace our vocation to join God in his good intention for creation

As I mentioned before, Marian and I decided that not only would I be non-combatant, I would be completely non-military. How could I be part of the military machine that continued to harass and suppress the very people that God had called me to? Being a conscientious objector meant that I would refuse to comply with any requirement of the state that I participate in the armed forces. This was a serious decision. At that time, this was considered to be a crime in South Africa and the penalty was imprisonment—Marian was brave to make this choice with me. It was not a good career move and it seemed like insanity to most of our family and friends

31. Ibid., 42.
32. Ibid., 43.

at the time. In retrospect though, this decision was the one of the sanest decisions that I have ever made.

I was perhaps *out of* my mind in the eyes of some, but their opinion did not matter because I had to live with myself; I had to live out of *my own mind*. But more importantly, I needed to live on the bread that comes from the Father's mouth. I do not pretend that my experience was anything like that of Jesus, or others who paid the ultimate price in the battle against apartheid, but in some small way I too experienced the riskiness of knowing that I was called to join God in what he was doing in South Africa.

The months that followed my decision to become non-military were nerve-wracking. We expected that I would be arrested at any point, but for some unexplainable reason it never happened. Today, I know that in the liminal space we listen for the voice of the One who invites us to join him in his mission—and it give us the strength to push through. Wright is, again, very helpful when he remarks that:

> At the heart of our resistance to temptation is love and loyalty to the God who has already called us his beloved children in Christ, and who holds out before us the calling to follow him in the path which leads to the true glory. In that glory lies the true happiness, the true fulfilment, which neither world, nor flesh, nor devil can begin to imitate.[33]

Breaking open the stagnant pools of *subverted destiny and freedom* is also a part of the experience of those who follow God's storyline in *life that is in need of regeneration*. Christians are invited to join God in his mission to decommission the colonizing powers of sin and death. Our vocation is to be *activists* of God's coming reign.

David Bosch's vision of this is that what Christians "erect in the here and now, in the teeth of those structures, are signs of God's new world."[34] That is what Jesus did. When he returned from his ordeal in the desert, he declared his intention to agitate against the congealed pools of human existence. In his first public appearance, he read the words from the prophet Isaiah: "God's Spirit is on me; he's chosen me to preach the message of good news to the poor, sent me to announce pardon to prisoners and recovery of sight to the blind, to set the burdened and battered free, to announce, 'This is God's year to act.'"[35]

33. Wright, *Luke*, 45.

34. Bosch, *Transforming Mission*, 176.

35. Luke 4:18–19 (The Message).

We will do well to consider the ways of Jesus as we face our own liminality. Not only do we need to guard against losing our freedom in pursuit of careers, but we need to commit ourselves to a cause that is greater than ourselves. We need to live vocationally in this time of liminality. Since God wants to see his creation grow into what he intended it to be, the question becomes rather: What forms of service can I commit myself to that will lead to greater freedom? So much around us reminds us that this world is aching, yearning for freedom. I do not think I even need to list examples here. We can all come up with pages for ourselves. I am beginning to see, however, that when I work for freedom I am not only doing good, I am also worshipping the God who intended us to be free. So, *right practice* is to act in line with God's righteous processes.

Jesus demonstrated how we can discover and follow God's storyline in times of great uncertainty—in liminality. Today, we too need to find our way through and, like Jesus, we discern, internalize, and commit to live a life that will produce freedom around us. Lives that work against stagnation and fatedness, lives that are part of God's plan of regeneration.

Now for the Courage to Live the Story

The epic tales of the *Hobbit* and *Lord of the Rings* seem to be a timely warning of the dangers of living with the temptations that liminality presents. For those in middle earth—a picture of liminality—the ring embodies temptation. We see that when people succumb to the ring of power, when it is slipped over someone's knuckles, how they lose their way. Bilbo Baggins the hobbit becomes corrupt and Sméagol kills his best friend for it. Kingdoms rise in war and innocent lives are destroyed in one bloody battle after another.

We see in the story, however, how a fellowship of the ring—with the ring of power safely nestled in a community—ensures that the ring carrier does not succumb to the temptations of claiming the ring as his. It took a community, a fellowship, to carry the ring to be destroyed in the fires of Mordor. Frodo, who carries the ring to Mordor, is not the real hero. Rather it is Samwise the Brave who is the hero. Samwise, who stops Frodo from grabbing power and who helps Frodo stay on course.

It is in community that we find our way through liminality. As in Lord of the Rings, where there is a fellowship that works together, this community should be marked by love, not power. M. Scott Peck once defined love as "the will to extend one's self for the purpose of nurturing one's own or another's spiritual growth."[36] In some way this definition encapsulates the love of God—the Trinity extended itself and made space for us to grow. It seems quite logical, then, to argue that the love that flows through this relationship to us should also flow through us to others. As we seek to find our way through liminality, we ought to become more intentional about extending ourselves for others, creating room for them to live.

Jesus's temptation and J. R. R. Tolkien's fantasy confirm our own experience of the challenges we face in liminal living. It is not a space where we think about others first. It seems to be more intuitive to serve one's own interests here. But Jesus, especially, shows a different way through. These actions of Jesus are like signposts to help us discern the trajectory of the storyline of *regeneration*—helping us stay on track, enabling us to live our lives with a sense of vocation in the murkiness caused by the presence of both faith and unfaith in our lives.

As we commit ourselves to a life where loving God means that we prioritize making space for life, we begin to hear the whisperings of God's voice. As we commit ourselves to a life that avoids fatedness and encourages God's creation to come to its full potential, we can hear the voice of God breaking through. As we commit ourselves to being troubled by what God is troubled by, then the voice of God becomes perceptible—we embrace his mission and we can begin to live the dangerous adventure of a passionate God.

Along this path we will be tempted to follow old patterns of thought, we could easily miss the trajectory of the storyline that we are following and get stuck in traditionalism, pragmatism, dogmatism, and faddism. Our minds need to be renewed every day, and to this we now turn.

36. Peck, *Road Less Traveled*, 81.

8

Trajectory Minding

Being Re-Minded by the Story

We quickly discovered how murky the socio-political conditions really were on our return to South Africa in the mid-1980s. It would have been very easy for us to slip back into a hierarchical view of society; a view where I (as a white Afrikaner male) could insist on the so-called superiority of my race and gender.

It would have been easy to justify how a system like apartheid could have been conceived. It could be easy to have sympathy for the Europeans who first arrived at the tip of Africa. They encountered a world that was not anything like the Europe they had left behind. Apart from the need for physical survival, farming in antipodean conditions, they also needed to overcome the mental obstacles of identity and purpose. In short, like all of us today, they needed to make sense of their new world—to find coherence between what they believed and how to live it out in this new land. Salman Rushdie in his third novel, *Shame*, reflects on the unique mental challenges that migrants face. He writes:

> When individuals come unstuck from their native land, they are called migrants. When nations do the same (Bangladesh), the act is called secession. What is the best thing about migrant peoples are seceded nations? I think it is their hopefulness. . . . And what's the worst thing? It is the emptiness of one's luggage. I'm speaking of invisible suitcases, not the physical, perhaps cardboard, variety containing a few meaning-drained mementoes: we have come

> unstuck from more than land. We have floated upwards from history from memory, from Time.[1]

Marian and I could certainly sympathize with them. We found ourselves in a whole new world as we settled into our new lives with people who had been victims of apartheid. In addition to my teaching and leadership role at the college, we were appointed leaders of a small church in an area that was considered "grey," because the government could not relocate all the colored people from this suburb. In addition, we also accepted a call to direct the ministry to street kids in Cape Town. Our adjustment was nothing in comparison to the first migrants; maybe we could appreciate their anxieties as they tried to survive.

As I mentioned before, for those of us who were born and nurtured under apartheid in South Africa, the notion of segregation was etched into our collective subconscious as a holy and fundamental principle of life. In these early days we could easily have slipped back into that worldview again. Maybe our alternative lifestyle was tantamount to questioning God? And maybe we were finding fault with how he had determined things to be? Were we out of our minds? There were times that we seriously questioned our sanity and were tempted to walk away. We realized then, that our minds still needed to be renewed every day. That an experience like the one what we had in the United States is only the beginning. We would still need to be re-minded by our story and the Story we find ourselves in—everyday.

Mind the Tension

In retrospect, I can see that we are re-minded by the Story when we struggle to keep the tension between our beliefs and our practices, between the cultural questions and traditional answers. This is where we do theology. When there are incongruencies, we should look for ways to make sense of them. This is at the heart of generative theology. To abdicate, to walk away from it, would have catastrophic consequences. We would claim one thing and live as if we do not believe it, and in the process we become practical atheists. Paul Stevens explains, "Might not the most pernicious heresy in the church today be the disharmony between those who claim to

1. Rushdie, *Shame*, 91.

be theologically approved but live as practical atheists?"[2] This is a situation not uncommon in the church today.

This became very clear to me in early 1990 when, as a thirty-year-old pastor, I led our small congregation through a season of contrition for our complicity in apartheid. During that time, we also had an influx of new members and most of them came from disadvantaged communities. It was already difficult for people to integrate, but matters became more complicated with the arrival of kids from the Boys Home. These kids were rough; they survived the streets of Cape Town. Some of them had been involved in gangs, with drugs, with prostitution, but all of them had been abused or abandoned. While we were not a wealthy congregation by any stretch of the imagination, we would have been a five-star upgrade for all of them.

Most of the church members were uncomfortable with their presence. At first sight of the boys, many mothers would pull their children closer, while their husbands would quickly slip out to see if their car doors were locked. Even though many of these boys became followers of Jesus in this time, their personal hygiene did not immediately improve, prompting some ladies to bring deodorized handkerchiefs to church.

After a while there was a consensus; these young men were not welcome. A delegation of the church council cornered me after an evening worship service with this ultimatum: "Pastor, they will have to go. And if you don't agree, you will have to go with them." But from the back of the pack came a question, a sacred question. Joe was not part of the delegation, but because he had an acquired brain injury he perhaps did not realize what was going on. On that day, his handicap was a gift to this young pastor. "Pastor," he asked, "if the boys go, where will Jesus go?" My accusers left me stunned by the sacredness of the question and, as time passed, the church became one of the first integrated communities in our denomination. I silently agreed with the theological truism that "the church without the handicapped is a handicapped church."

Theology that is generative will embrace the uncertainties that arise out of the tension between our beliefs and behaviors and re-mind those who practice it. I knew by then that theology can become a dominant monolith that pretends to have all the answers, or even the ability to predict all the questions that people might ask, now and forever, when it ignores the blatant incongruence between the beliefs and the behaviors that it sponsors. Then it has become a locked cage and the key is in the hands

2. Stevens, *Other Six Days*, 254.

of the powerful few. Then the faith that it spawns colonizes the faithful as much as it colonizes the continent that it conquered.

Instead of helping us find meaning, it imposes meaning just as European colonialism imposed a way of life on the first-people of the continent. Instead of becoming the conduit of truth, it becomes the enforcer of its brand of *faith*—with all of its traditionalism, dogmatism, and pragmatism in tow. (See diagram below).

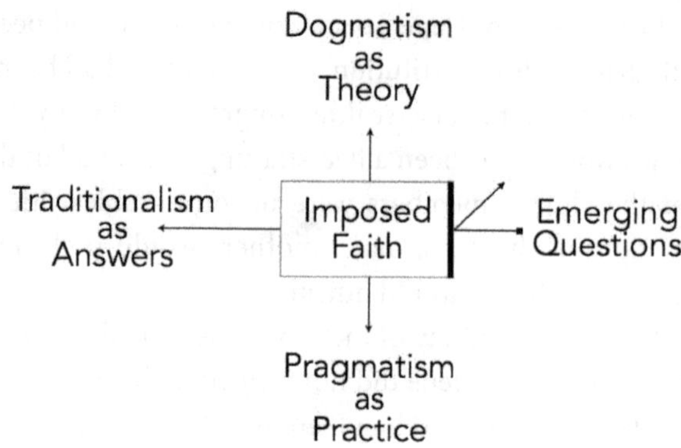

If we are denied the freedom to find our faith for ourselves, if we are not free to question the incongruencies of our lives, we will soon find that faith produces dogmas and not vibrant beliefs, pragmatism and not thoughtful actions. The living traditions of the champions of the Christian faith become a dead traditionalism and those who dare ask the obvious questions are branded heretics. G. K. Chesterton rightly warned, "Dogma[3] does not mean the absence of thought, but the end of thought."[4] The delusion exists that when we silence the questions, we will have peace. What we in fact end up with is the pretence of meaning. Michel Foucault insightfully declares that "power is knowledge"[5] in this case. Traditions are now interpreted in the light of this so-called truth and a dead traditionalism is created. Behaviors are now monitored and policed to ensure that people live within the dogmatism and traditionalism of the theological system. In this close-minded system, no unsolicited questions can be tolerated. We will return to this in more detail below.

3. In dogmatism, something is true because someone in power says that it is true.

4. Chesterton, *Victorian Age*, 15.

5. Foucault, *Critical Theory*, 133.

Mind the Trajectory

We are re-minded by the Story as we discern and follow the trajectory of the story. The trajectory of God's story, which curves away from colonization and one-upmanship, served as a way to interpret what was happening around us, and that helped us to find our way through a very dangerous passage of time in South Africa in the 1990s. I realized that, as a participant in this story of regeneration, I could never again live life as if Easter did not happen; I had to allow the reality of Easter to re-mind me every day.

As much as it was true that there were slaves in most of the Old Testament (Act 2 of our story) there was a shift after Easter. Now masters are called upon to treat their slaves with dignity, and ultimately to set them free. That requires that I too treat everyone as my equal. It might be true that women were treated badly in most of the Old Testament, but there was a shift after Easter when women became the first witnesses to Jesus's resurrection. This was a big deal in a world where women could not be witnesses in a court of law. There is even evidence that a woman instructed a man in theology.[6] How outrageous! The trajectory is clear: it points towards Paul's vision: "In Christ's family there can be no division into Jew and non-Jew, slave and free, male and female. Among us you are all equal."[7]

God is a dynamic being who is on a mission in this world and theology that has God as its subject could therefore not be a static, academic exercise. God's action in this world is on a trajectory, and through faithful theology we attempt to discern that trajectory. Georg Vicedom says that "when we ascribe the mission to God in this way, then it is withdrawn from human whims."[8] We participate in God's sending of his Son in his mission. Vicedom reminds us that "the missionary movement of which we are a part has its source in the triune God himself."[9] And if the world is constantly changing, and if God is doing a new thing in this changing world, then it is to be expected that God will also challenge our thinking. Theology, by definition, can therefore not be static; it cannot be like a locked room or a bird in a cage, it must be more like a bird in flight. I agree completely with Charles Gerkin's understanding of the task of theology when he says that theology is:

6. Acts 18:24–26.
7. Gal 3:28 (The Message).
8. Vicedom, *Mission of God*, 5.
9. Ibid.

> the critical and constructive reflection on the life and work of Christians in all the varied contexts in which that life takes place with the intention of facilitating transformation of life in all its dimensions in accordance with the Christian gospel.[10]

Mind One-Upmanship

We are re-minded by the Story of God who allowed death in himself to occur. Abuse of power, as demonstrated in the varied forms of one-upmanship, is, I believe, a prime cause and consequence of stagnation in the church. Jesus despised one-upmanship; it was what Gentile rulers did. Jesus thrashed the leader-follower divide. He would have nothing to do with the ancient notion of being a king who lorded it over his subjects. Unfortunately, the church does not seem to be immune to the danger of power in liminal living. It has tragically succumbed to it on occasion and ecclesiastical structures have often ensconced knowledge in power.

This is not how the Godhead behaves.

In the act of creating beings in his image, there is consultation and a council meeting in the Godhead. Scripture says, "God said let *us* create people in *our* image." The power is in the Godhead, not wrapped up in the Father alone. The church rejected the heresy of subordinationism, a view that suggests that there is hierarchy in the Trinity, a long time ago.[11] There is no one-up-Father-ship in the Godhead. Power is shared equally; authority belongs to all three persons of the trinitarian community—of Father, Son, and Holy Spirit.

It is hard to imagine what life would be like without domination, without one-upmanship. The Garden does, however, give us a picture of this kind of life; of humanity *in our generative state* in the garden. Here, relationships existed where power is the product of *oneness* and *honor*.

The Trinity is a beautiful example of oneness. If we have seen the Son we have seen the Father. The Holy Spirit is, historically, the bond that personifies the love between the Father and Son. The notion of oneness is fundamental to our understanding of God.

10. Gerkin, *Widening the Horizons*, 61.

11. A doctrine that suggests that Son or Holy Spirit is inferior to the Father in the Trinity.

Oneness is also God's intention for human relationships; this is how it started with Adam and Eve. Eve is taken from the man's side as a poetic gesture of the special relationship of the genders and of humanity.

Honor is an acknowledgement of the uniqueness of every person in the Godhead. In a similar way, there is honor in human relationships as we acknowledge that we need each other in order to be our best. This is what Africans call *ubuntu*. *Ubuntu* summarizes my understanding of honor in relationships and demonstrates God's intention for humanity:

> *Ubuntu* means that they are generous, hospitable, friendly, caring and compassionate. They share what they have. It also means my humanity is caught up, is inextricably bound up, in theirs. We belong in a bundle of life. We say, "a person is a person through other people." It is not "I think therefore I am." It says rather: "I am human because I belong. I participate, I share." A person with *ubuntu* is open and available to others, does not feel threatened that others are able and good; for he or she has a proper self-assurance that comes from knowing that he or she belongs in a greater whole and is diminished when others are humiliated or diminished, when others are tortured or oppressed, or treated as if they were less than who they are.[12]

It comes as no surprise, then, that God did not give authority to Adam alone. It seems that the dictum "Absolute power corrupts, absolutely"[13] was not an eighteenth-century insight after all. That is why authority was given to a couple. We read:

> So God created man in his own image, in the image of God he created him; male and female he created them. God blessed them and said to them, "Be fruitful and increase in number; fill the earth and subdue it. Rule over the fish of the sea and the birds of the air and over every living creature that moves on the ground."[14]

It was only after the fall that power entered human relationships and Eve was told, "Your desire will be for your husband and he will rule over you." This is the unfortunate situation that prevails throughout the Old Testament, leaving in its wake slavery, polygamy, and monarchy. Lives wasted by prejudice and minds twisted by power.

12. Tutu, *No Future*, 35.

13. Attributed to John Emerich Edward Dalberg Acton, first Baron Acton (1834–1902).

14. Gen 1:27–28 (NIV).

The mind can so easily be imprisoned by power. When this happens to me and I am unwilling or unable to move in my thinking, I find that pride is lurking in the shadows. My reluctance to see my own self-interest thwarted and frustrated is often the cause for oppression and suffering for others; this, I have come to appreciate, is a universal human weakness.

Because societies and cultures are often fuelled by nationalistic pride, oppression and injustice can easily be spotted in the history of nations. We are deluding ourselves to think that the systems of the political system in the world today are able or even willing to provide principles either for the elimination of oppression or for the eradication of injustice. Any attempt to remove a situation of oppression will soon run afoul of somebody's self-interests. In practice, structures will change only to the degree that is necessary for survival, and they will then continue on exactly the same lines as before.[15]

Mind Thinking

We are re-minded by the Story one thought and feeling at a time. Eugene Peterson gets the gist of it when he paraphrases Paul's words: "The world is unprincipled. It's dog-eat-dog out there! The world doesn't fight fair." Yet Paul is optimistic about how followers of Jesus treat those in and outside the church. According to Paul, "We don't live or fight our battles that way. Our weapons are not carnal," he says.[16]

Carnality points to our fallen way of existence. It is an existence where we want to achieve one-upmanship. The carnal way is to subdue and to dominate; it is to manipulate, out-maneuver, and cajole. But because of Easter there is a new path, a new approach that will lead to the regeneration of all of creation. Eugene Peterson says, "The tools of our trade aren't for marketing or manipulation, but they are for demolishing that entire massively corrupt culture." Paul explains how we get out of this place of carnal thinking, which is like a stronghold or prison, when he writes, "We demolish arguments and every pretension that sets itself up against the knowledge of God and we take captive every thought to make it obedient to Christ."[17] We are being re-minded in this way.

15. I first came across these thoughts in the 1980s. This paragraph reflects the thoughts of Reid, "Preaching," 10ff.

16. 2 Cor 10:3–5 (The Message).

17. 2 Cor 10:5 (NIV).

Sometimes it feels as if we Christians are not very different from others when it comes to the strength of our self-interest and opinions. Paul uses the picture of a prison to illustrate the carnal way of thinking because such thinking always leads to imprisonment. There seem to be three steps to the way our thinking becomes captive to something other than Christ: (1) Thoughts are not submitted to Christ; (2) such thoughts exalt themselves; and finally (3) these become a form of logic. It is a mind bending away from Christ.

We cannot control ideas from entering our minds. This is as true as acknowledging that we cannot stop a bird from flying over our heads, but just as we can make a choice to stop a bird from making a nest in our hair, however, the feelings that come with thoughts are more complicated to control. Thoughts and feelings are inseparable[18] in the choices that we make and as such thoughts and their accompanying feelings cluster. In the world of birds it is said that "birds of a feather flock together"; this is also true for thoughts and feelings. There is a particular cluster of thoughts (read thoughts and feelings) that concerns Paul—it is the types of thoughts that erect barriers against the truth of God. He chooses the Greek word *hupsoma* in this text, which means that something is elevated. This could be translated here as "the exaltation" or "the tower." Paul is saying that our thoughts can become towers of arrogance and pride. This reminds me of what we have already noted in an earlier chapter in our discussion of pride. Pride is the first step we take on our journey of *unfaith*; it is the act that signals that we are taking matters into our own hands. So, in the Christian classics pride is deadly. It marches first in the parade of deadly sins.

From this *tower*, arguments develop and ways of thinking become entrenched in our mind. It is like a heavy ball that is being rolled into a sandpit. At first the ball will stop short, but after many attempts a delta forms at the entry point and deep grooves develop, allowing the thoughts to run further and faster. The scarier part of this image is that the delta forces thoughts that are slightly off its course into the same groove. I think this is what Paul had in mind when he referred to arguments—logic that has its origin in pride. We run into difficulty and we end up being stuck in a rut or, as Paul the Apostle imagines, a prison. It is obvious that ways of thinking that originate in proud thoughts will lead to incarceration. Places that are the billabongs, the hot rock pools of life. We could illustrate this as follows:

18. This idea is well developed by Willard, *Renovation*, chapter 2.

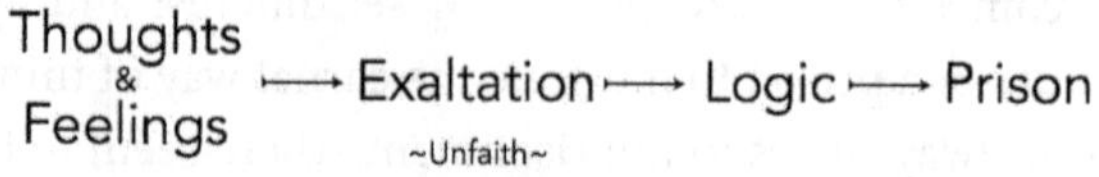

Thoughts & Feelings ⟶ Exaltation ⟶ Logic ⟶ Prison
~Unfaith~

I already pointed out that when our traditional answers, current theories, and practices become towers of pride,[19] we become less willing to engage questions that could renew the way we make sense of this world. Then power becomes knowledge and faith, a form of colonization. If there is no space for sacred questions, then faith—as seeking and constructing meaning—is reduced to a form of godliness without the power to transform. It is reduced to unfaith. It is also true, however, that we can become so enamored with questions for the sake of questions, that the obsession with the latest theories and practices becomes a logic that drives us to faddism—this might be a hip prison, but it is still a prison and another expression of unfaith. The sad result of this unfaith is that we ignore the trajectory of the Story that we find ourselves in and we end up with twisted minds that imprison us in traditionalism, dogmatism, pragmatism, and faddism.

Mind Traditionalism

If questions are not handled with care, the tension between the traditional answers and the emerging questions can produce this prison in which we cannot be re-minded by the Story. The way I see it, traditional answers are like a treasure chest. These are the things we have learned from other people, books, and experiences. We draw on this treasure chest to develop faith content to enable us to live and make our practical commitments. At the same time we are challenged every day to answer new questions, questions that we often do not have answers for. By ignoring these questions, we may find immediate but short-term relief. The tensions go away and we can relax. We all need to do this from time to time; I guess that is why we take holidays. If, however, this becomes a way of life, our unwillingness to deal with the new questions will be like unused calories that turn into the fat of pride.

19. Though pride is the one ingredient that would weaken and even dissolve the binding power of faith-seeking-meaning (*fides quaerens*), it is not true that unreasonable certainty is always associated with pride.

When I am so certain that I am right, when things have become so clear that it destroys my ability to see, then I will refuse to entertain new questions. When we get to this place we have to develop complex systems to contain truth and ensure that our version of reality remains unaffected by tides of change in society. This is what we have also come to know as traditionalism. The great religious historian Jaroslav Pelikan once said, and I think it can hardly be said more succinctly, that "tradition is the living faith of the dead; traditionalism is the dead faith of the living."[20]

Traditionalism becomes overly certain about its stance. It ignores the conflicting bits of information and a version of reality is constructed with neat categories and beliefs. Whatever fits into my system is recognized and accepted, whatever does not is ignored.

I have been fortunate to see many beautiful cities in the world. In early 2000, I was invited to join a group of ministers in Kiev. It would be my first trip to a country that once was part of the Soviet Union. I was very excited. One of the highlights of our stay was our visit to the Pechersk Lavra on the Dnipro Hills. This is arguably one of the greatest church and museum complexes in the world. This compound of churches and other architectural masterpieces has been standing for nearly a thousand years, providing a sacred space for many worshippers to encounter God.

Standing in a church that was not of the same tradition that I was from, I wondered like many of my students, "Why am I here? What could I learn from a tradition so foreign and distant?" It was obvious that the other ministers who were with me had similar thoughts and questions. Some of them became quite giddy with discomfort as the fathers of this congregation led a small band of believers in worship. Others pointed to the many adornments on the walls and commented about the extravagance, fearing that it was a form of idolatry. My experience was, however, quite different because from where I was standing, I could see a young veiled woman in deep worship, her eyes moist in prayer, her head bowed in submission. There was no doubt in my mind that her heart was open to God.

Whilst I am not an expert on the Russian Orthodox Church, I know that, like other traditions, it has its own strengths and weaknesses. But this experience highlighted how excessively certain we can be that we are right and that others who do not think, see, or act like us must be wrong.

I recently learned that a frog could starve to death in a heap of flying insects. As long as these insects remain still, the frog's eyes cannot detect

20. Pelikan, *Christian Tradition*, 9.

them, so they are safe. As soon as they become active and try to fly away, the frog's eye is programmed to detect that motion and its tongue is trained to snap out in pursuit of its meal. In the same way, we can become conditioned to see only what we want to see. We will then avoid the questions that our traditional answers cannot address and our traditionalism will not answer. If this goes on for long enough then, like the frog, we could die of starvation.

Mind Dogmatism

We noted earlier that G. K. Chesterton warns: "Dogma does not mean the absence of thought, but the end of thought."[21] In dogmatism something is true because someone in power says that it is true. In this space it is difficult to be re-minded by the Story. When I first encountered the trap of dogmatism I was barely twenty years old, a student doing my undergraduate studies in a pre-theology course. After my encounter with Bishop Tutu during his public lecture, my world began to unravel. I was not doing well spiritually at this time.

Somehow, I still ended up on the local church council of the church of my childhood. The first thing I was given as a member of the council was a green vinyl folder that contained the faith practice and procedures of the denomination we belonged to. Over the next few weeks I became a student of the rules, clauses, and sub-clauses of this very important document.

A crisis moment that is imprinted on my memory forever took place at that time. I was sitting in a church council meeting with all the other members listening to the reasons for the dismissal of the youth minister. It was common knowledge then, that the senior pastor's son was finishing his studies at Bible College and would need some employment soon. That night, to my shame, I used very strong language to make my own dogmatic position clear. I was dogmatic in my view that the dismissal was a blatant abuse of the constitution to enforce nepotism. Afrikaans (my mother tongue) is as expressive as Dutch, and it enabled me to hit the ceiling with disgust. At the same time, the senior pastor dogmatically stated his theological justifications for centralized and hierarchical leadership in the church. My anger boiled over and I uttered expletives that I am too embarrassed to put in print. I was never asked to repent and the youth pastor was

21. Chesterton, *Victorian Age*, 15.

still dismissed to make way for the new appointment. We both suffered the consequences of a bended mind.

Dogmatism also manifests in other ways and could easily be mistaken for thoughtfulness. To say that a person is dogmatic is to imply that the person has thought through the matter and has come to some firm conclusions. Dogmatism is, however, often exactly the opposite of being thoughtful. At best, it seems one can say the person once thought about the matter, settled it, and now believes that no further thinking is required. If we feel we have already found the answer, there is no room for wondering or further exploration. In fact, in some faith communities further exploration would be seen as a sign of spiritual decline, or even worse, of spiritual death.

To my mind the opposite seems equally true. A community that encourages thought and theological questioning could be opening the door to stronger doctrines, more courageous practices, and a deeper commitment to the traditions that they hold. Is it better to fence questions or rather to create a safe place for dialogue about the issues of faith and life? I propose the latter as a strategy.

If we engage the tough questions in critical yet constructive ways, we will grow beyond the unreasonable answers we have been dishing up in the name of orthodoxy. Surely, the church as the safest place on earth can make space for faith-seeking-meaning?

Mind Pragmatism

In the early 1990s, a young Old Testament professor felt that he was called to make a prophetic statement about the state of the church in his city. He was part of a denomination that had been through a painful split forty years earlier. The two denominations continued to exist side by side in a small U.S. town in the Deep South. The one became very strong in its doctrine, while the other placed emphasis on holiness practices. He went to the local hardware store and bought the biggest axe handle that he could find. On the one end he wrote "Church of dogmatism" and on the other side he wrote, "Church of pragmatism." He broke the handle in two to symbolize how this church was broken in two by the political fallout of many years ago. Over the next few months he carried this broken axe handle—that he had mended with electrician's tape—wherever he went. When he was asked what he was doing, he would speak about the broken state of his denomination, with its symptoms of dogmatism and pragmatism. Ricky knew that the Story cannot re-mind us if we are in the trap of dogmatism and pragmatism.

I remember the impact this story had on me in the early 1990s when I was trying to stand up against apartheid in the church of my childhood. I longed to have the same courage to act prophetically to break the pragmatism of my own denomination. This denomination had four churches for four people groups in South Africa—this was seen as a very practical thing to do. But the white church had control over the constitution of the denomination and basically determined the future of the so-called Colored, Black, and Indian Churches. When our denomination was asked if it would support the apartheid policy of the new government, they received the answer, "Don't worry about us; we already practice apartheid in the church."

I was barely thirty years old and newly ordained when I found myself in a General Council Meeting where all the pastors of this denomination gathered to debate the merits of apartheid in the church. It is hard to imagine that we did that, but this was a hot topic in the 1980s and 1990s in South Africa.

In a heated debate at the General Council Meeting, I wanted to know what theology underpinned our practice of segregation in the church. To this day, I am stunned by the callous pragmatism that was reflected in the answer: "There is no theology; it works." That is pragmatism in its essence: it must be right if it works. In my youthful exuberance and theological desperation I pursued the point until a denominational theologian in residence explained the pragmatic approach. "A husband and a wife," he said, "can be spiritually one but live in two different houses." We can therefore be one with our non-white church, but not live in the same house. For years after the demise of apartheid, this denomination continued with its apartheid policies, it resisted the trajectory of the Story that we find ourselves in.

Mind Faddism

A trap that is equally dangerous is the trap of *faddism*. If pragmatism says that something is right because it works, then faddism says that something is right because it is new. Here too, we may find it hard to be re-minded by the Story. In an attempt to be relevant and up to date, there is a disregard for those who have gone before and who have also attempted to be faithful in their own time and contexts. In the name of progression, and in an attempt to be relevant, we can so engage the emerging questions that we forget to draw on the "living faith of the dead"—tradition.

When we fall into the trap of fads, we soon discover it is a never-ending cycle. It is like standing between two mirrors where one reflection creates another and there is a string of images projected into a seeming eternity. I have noticed that within hours of buying the latest and coolest piece of equipment, I often become immediately dissatisfied when my attention is drawn to something even more cool and hip. Fads produce fads, and in their wake follows unhappiness, which can only be silenced by something new. Someone once said, "Half the world is unhappy because they can't have the things that are making the other half unhappy."

As I mentioned before, apartheid seemed reasonable to me as a child and for a few brief years as an adult, but a culmination of experiences revealed the cracks in the Afrikaner story. It became incoherent for me as a worldview and I finally needed to act on my convictions that apartheid was evil. As a consequence, Marian and I made the cultural leap from apartheid and we committed ourselves to the so-called colored people of Cape Town. We rejected the doctrines, practices, and the traditions of apartheid. It was a new world that no one could have prepared us for. In my naiveté I must have believed that we would be accepted without suspicion, that we would have no dogmatism, traditionalism, and pragmatism in this new world. I was mistaken—very soon we were embracing a new dogmatism, traditionalism, and pragmatism. But this time it was one inspired by a disdain for apartheid. I was now convinced that anyone who was still in the white church had to be racist, which radically reduced my circle of influence.

Mind mending

If, however, faith is truly about making sense of the world we live in, then it is the glue that holds the *quadpolarity* of questions, answers, theory, and practice together. The courageous act of questioning is a vital ingredient of a vibrant faith; in this space we are re-minded by the Story. Without sacred questions there is no tension, and meaning evaporates.

Faith that seeks meaning will ask reasonable questions that will take seriously the doubts that are generated by the inefficiencies of our current theories, doctrines, and practices. At the same time, faith that seeks meaning will attempt to answer these questions through the certainty that comes from traditional theories and practices—while exposing answers that have become unreasonable. Through this process of question and answer we end up with new insights that could lead to richer theory, doctrines, and possibly more courageous practices. Faith that seeks meaning will continue this process by insisting that the content of our faith and its practice cohere.

I know from my own experience, however, that I often end up in places that are emotionally dark, places that feel like the shadows in one of Caravaggio's paintings or the basement of Pitts Theological Library. A place far from home, in a prison, and it is all on account of pride that is at work in me. There are also times when I feel that I have the answers and that my theories enable me to live faithfully every day. I have noticed, however, that when I become complacent and ignore the new questions that life dishes up, my theories turn into dogmas, my practices turn into dead routines, and my answers turn into laws. I have also noticed that I can be tempted to chase fads in order to escape the mind-numbing drudgery of my dogmas, routines, and laws. It could be a new idea or a new approach or a new answer that could provide that temporary relief—but this too is a prison. I have found it helpful to speak of four prisons, or traps, that I find myself in.

According to Paul, we can avoid going to jail. The original language in the text from 2 Corinthians is interesting in that the word for prison can also be a fortress, a home. There is a fork in the road; there is better route. The big difference is that we can build towers that are characterized not by pride, but by obedience to Christ. What this means is that our thoughts can be shaped by the story of God in Christ through faith. Paul uses a military term—he says Christians "take captive every thought to make it obedient to Christ."[22] In the same way that soldiers would use their spears to bring the enemy under their control (an image that is far too violent for my non-violent sensibilities), Christians ought to bring their thoughts under control in Christ.

Peterson's translation captures this well. He says that Christians use their tools to fit "every loose thought and emotion and impulse into the structure of life shaped by Christ."[23] Followers of Christ follow logic too, but it is a logic that is guided by the Story that we find ourselves in, the story of the God's regeneration of his creation. And because we have direct access to this story through Jesus, our thoughts are brought in line with his thoughts. The Word, according to Fowler, is "the structure of reason, wisdom, and

22. 2 Cor 10:5 (NIV).

23. 2 Cor 10:5 (The Message).

lawfulness" that is "built into the very heart of everything." He explains it in full when he writes:

> In the Christian classic there is a long tradition that links the Logos—the word of God, the wisdom of God, the eternal Christ of God—with creation. . . . We understand the Logos in creation as the structure that intends righteousness in the processes of history. The Logos is a structure, a reason, wisdom, and lawfulness built into the very heart of things. It is designed to guide and lure the interplay of destiny and freedom towards God's intended future.[24]

This way of thinking takes us to a place of safety; it takes us home. Our diagram can be expanded to capture this fork in the road:

~Unfaith~
Thoughts & Feelings → Exaltation → Logic → Prison
Thoughts & Feelings → Logos → Logic → Home
~Faith~

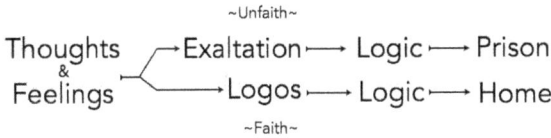

At a national level in South Africa we could see what Fowler meant when he wrote that "the Logos in creation as the structure that intends righteousness in the processes of history."[25] On February 2, 1990, when F. W. de Klerk, the last South African President under apartheid, opened Parliament, he stunned the world. Most people expected the same old rhetoric. De Klerk was regarded as a conservative from a staunch National Party family. I remember also teaching at a so-called Colored University (as if being the Dean of a Bible College, pastoring a local church, and directing a home for street kids was not enough) when he was Minister of Education, and he was ultra-conservative then. But on that historic, bewildering Friday he announced that it was in the interest of all to end apartheid and to establish "a new and just constitutional dispensation in which every inhabitant will enjoy equal rights, treatment and opportunity." He was declaring the end of apartheid. The African National Congress and other political organizations were unbanned, political prisoners were released, various security regulations abolished, and Nelson Mandela would be released as soon as possible to play an important part.

24. Fowler, *Faith Development*, 43.

25. Ibid.

A lot has been written about F. W. de Klerk's motivations.[26] Why did he do this? Why would he give up power and risk being accused a traitor by his own people? In a recent interview on CNN he explained that apartheid was birthed in a time when "in America and elsewhere, and across the continent of Africa, there was still not this realization that we are trampling upon the human rights of people. So I'm a convert." His mind changed when he realized that apartheid was unjust.[27] The Story that we find ourselves in, the story of God's regeneration of his creation, is a story of how God empowers the powerless and how he restores justice to this world. I do not know if F. W. de Klerk was even aware of this, but when he embraced the sacred question of the injustices wrought by apartheid, and he decided to do something with that, he joined God in his mission to bring justice. He was re-minded by the Story. De Klerk demonstrated that freedom is possible—that we can escape dogmatism, pragmatism, traditionalism, and faddism if we are willing to embrace the questions that need to be answered when we lay aside our pride and open a conversation.[28]

26. See Ottaway, *Chained Together*, 68–71 for a discussion of de Klerk's complex motivation for reform.

27. My comments refer to the interactions between F. W. de Klerk and Nelson Mandela, two leaders during the first phase of their relationship, which extends roughly from February 1990 to the 1994 presidential election. Interview with Amanpour on May 12, 2012. Sadly, during this interview F. W. de Klerk could not agree that apartheid was morally repugnant, perhaps an indication that our minds are in the process of being renewed. See http://edition.cnn.com/ 2012/05/12/world/africa/south-africa-de-klerk/index.html.

28. For a full account, see http://capetown.at/heritage/history/newSA_mandela.htm.

9

New Mind

The Significance of Generosity

In the mid-1990s, as we were preparing for the elections, I became the acting principal of the college. The principal, who generously made space for me to work alongside him as an Afrikaner, had become ill and he needed to take an extended break from the stresses of work. The college faced many challenges: it was located in Athlone on the Cape Flats not far from where the notorious Trojan Horse Massacre[1] occurred in 1985. Athlone was filled with tension and the college was in the middle of it. From our campus we could see the armored vehicles of the South African Police and Defence Force storming onto the school campus across the way, shooting at the brothers, sisters, family, and friends of some of our students. We could see young people wandering onto streets, stoning cars, setting up barricades, and finding ways to vent their frustration and rage.

1. The South African Broadcast Corporation reports the findings of the Truth and Reconciliation Commission findings: "On 15 October 1985, members of the South African Railway Police hid in wooden crates on the back of a railway truck and opened fire on a crowd of protesters in Athlone, Cape Town, killing three youths and injuring several others. The operation was planned and implemented by a sub-structure of the regional Joint Management Centre. It was repeated in Crossroads, Cape Town, the following day, killing a further two youths." http://sabctrc.saha.org.za/ glossary/ trojan_horse_incident_cape_town.htm?tab=victims, accessed February 13, 2013. Actual footage of this event can still be found on the internet, see http://www.youtube .com/ watch?v=3qxwdJoz1vo.

During this anxious time, I needed to be re-minded by the Story more than ever before. One morning, as I was preparing for the new academic year—a year that I knew would be exhilarating and more dangerous because of the elections—a distressed African student stepped into my office. "Sir," he said, "I was in a fight with another student." He was shaking as told me what happened. He had lost his temper with the hostel monitor and slapped him, cracking his inner ear. Fortunately for him, his victim laid no charges against him. But through a disciplinary hearing of the college board it was decided that he could not graduate that year, since graduates needed to be Christ-like in character. The college board agreed to graduate him in the future, and they did after he received counselling for his anger. The student was saddened by the news, but accepted it knowing that he did not have to also face a civil lawsuit.

I was just settling down after the rough start to the year when I received a phone call from an irate journalist who had just returned from exile. He had heard about what happened at the college and he was very certain that we were committing an injustice. He did not want to meet me, he did not want to see the multi-cultural nature of our college nor did he want to know about our commitment to the anti-apartheid struggle. He only wanted a comment from me. After thirty minutes of discussion on the phone, the reporter concluded that I had declined to comment. His mind was made up: all Afrikaner leaders were racists and I was one of them.

He would have been right if he met me before my encounter with James. By now it is old news that as a young Afrikaner I once believed that God forced non-white South Africans onto arid soil while he "blessed" Afrikaners with rich agricultural land. I once believed that the Übermensch rules over those who cannot rule over themselves. I once believed in the superiority of the Afrikaner as the Aryan race. But for years now, I had been re-minded by the Story that I find myself in, and by now that Story was changing my mind and heart.

He would not have known what I had already discovered in seminary, that Genesis 1:28 does not refer to unity within an ethnic group, but rather that this verse carries the idea of the unity of humankind.[2]

He would not have known that reading Karl Barth had convinced me that there were no nations in the time between Adam and Noah.[3] The intention of Genesis 1:28 is to describe humankind's commission to replenish

2. von Rad, *Old Testament Theology*, 173.

3. Barth, *Church Dogmatics*, 351.

the earth and to have dominion over the creatures that God had placed on the earth. There was no mention of nations dominating nations. This only occurs after the Fall in Genesis 3. I knew that apartheid usurped the space that God created for all of humanity and made it the privileged domain of a minority group in South Africa.

He would not have known that I had already seen the soft, selfish underbelly of apartheid that people like Beyers Naude, David Bosch, Bishop Tutu, and Allan Boesak revealed. Allan Boesak already convinced me that apartheid did not exclude black South Africans from the benefits of the land to ensure that the different nations had equal opportunity for development. Instead, subjugation was the more sinister purpose of this exclusion.[4]

He would not have known that for many years after my experience with James in America, I longed to go back to my family, friends, and the security and the certainty of apartheid; but there was no going back to the old way of thinking and living. He would not know that I was being reminded by the Story I found myself in and a new, generous frame of mind was emerging.

Generosity of Mind

A new way of thinking, a new frame of mind was required and Nelson Mandela and F. W. de Klerk demonstrated how this could be done. Their example gave us all hope, and still gives us hope today.[5] The history of South Africa will tell the story of the generosity of these two strong-willed men who escaped the prison of their traditional thinking and found a new way. They took their thoughts captive, perhaps they did it consciously in the name of Christ and perhaps they did not. But that still does not change the fact that their actions were shaped by the redemptive trajectory of the story in which humanity finds itself.

I cannot help but think that these two men, perhaps unknowingly, also responded to Paul the apostle's advice to church leaders: "Let your gentleness be evident to all."[6]

4. Boesak, "He made Us," 4.

5. My comments refer to the interactions between F. W. de Klerk and Nelson Mandela as two leaders during the first phase of their relationship, which extends roughly from February 1990 to the 1994 presidential election.

6. Phil 4:5 (NIV).

The Greek word for "gentleness"[7] receives a lot of attention when this passage is translated. Moises Silva indicates that gentleness should, however, not be confused for weakness when he writes, "Paul expects believers to be guided by a new frame of mind that does not put priority on personal rights."[8] This frame of mind was there from the beginning in Jesus, the Word of God. In a parallel passage in Philippians 2:1-4,[9] Paul pleads with the same church that they would be like-minded with Christ. He writes, "Then make my joy complete by being like-minded, having the same love, being one in spirit and of one mind. Do nothing out of selfish ambition or vain conceit. Rather, in humility value others above yourselves, not looking to your own interests but each of you to the interests of the others."[10]

During my seminary years I came across this definition of gentleness, which emphasizes that this frame of mind is about being generous in the face of adversity and danger. Fritz Reinecker says that "the word signifies a humble, patient steadfastness, which is able to submit to injustice, disgrace, and maltreatment without hatred or malice, trusting in God in spite of all of it."[11] Morna Hooker is on target in her comment that gentleness "denotes generosity toward others and is a characteristic of Christ himself." [12] This new frame of mind is a generosity of mind.

I am in no way suggesting that Mandela and de Klerk became best of friends, or that they even liked each other; they didn't. But the uniqueness of their relationship was clear to most South Africans and me. I had the privilege to defy apartheid laws when a non-white principal employed me as his academic dean in 1989, but what was happening between de Klerk and Mandela was rare. Examples of collaboration between former enemies who faced similar dilemmas to these two leaders are hard to find in history.[13]

7. The Greek word *epieikes* literally means: gentleness, graciousness.

8. Silva, *Philippians*, 194.

9. The Epistle to the Philipians is set out in a *chiastic* pattern. This pattern is a literary device that uses a unique repetition pattern for clarification and emphasis. In this pattern Philippians 1:27—2:4 and 4:1–5 are parallels.

10. Phil 2:2–4 (NIV).

11. Rienecker and Rogers, *Linguistic Key*, 560.

12. Hooker, *Letter to the Philippians*, 540.

13. See Glad, "Passing the Baton," 1–28.

Generosity Is Seen in Leaving—Being Present

When Mandela and de Klerk met in December 1989, they quickly knew that they could collaborate despite the clear differences that were there from the start. De Klerk insisted that white people had to be protected from majority rule, whereas Mandela knew that his followers would not be satisfied unless the "one man, one vote" principle was achieved.

Between 1989 and 1994, when the first post-apartheid election was held, they would walk the tight rope between meeting the expectations of their supporters and achieving their shared goal of a better future for everyone living in South Africa. But this would not be achieved if Mandela returned to his prison cell and de Klerk to his lofty presidential office. They would have to leave the known and familiar, risk their own formidable reputations, in order to be present with each other in a new space. In this new space there would not be room for greed, nor insistence on having it "my way or no way." Instead, a generous mind, which is humble, that demonstrates patient steadfastness in the face of insult and injury, which "seeks to understand before it makes itself understood," would need to prevail as they occupied this new space on the tight rope of democracy.

On February 2, 1990, not even three months after their famous first meeting, F. W. de Klerk stunned the South African parliament and the world with his announcement that he was releasing Nelson Mandela "unconditionally" and "without delay" as part of the sweeping political reform that he was initiating on that day. "History," he said as he finished his speech, "has placed a tremendous responsibility on the shoulders of this country's leadership, namely the responsibility of moving our country away from the current course of conflict and confrontation. . . ."[14]

A week later, Nelson Mandela walked free from his prison of twenty-seven years and he too was ready to engage his former enemy in a new space. The stalwarts of the African National Congress wrote most of the speech that he read to an adoring crowd of fifty thousand people who gathered at the Cape Town City Hall. But then he diverted from the party-line and called F. W. de Klerk "a man of integrity."[15] The next day, his intention to occupy the new space on the tight rope of democracy was even clearer when he acknowledged the fears and aspirations of white South Africans:

14. Foreign Broadcast Information Service, Africa, February 2, 1990, 10.

15. Ibid., February 12, 1990, 22.

> The ANC is very much concerned to address the question of the concerns of whites. They insist on structural guarantees to ensure that majority rule does not result in the domination of whites by blacks. We understand that fear. Whites are our fellow South Africans, and we want them to feel safe and to know that we appreciate the contribution that they have made toward the development of this country.[16]

Both leaders left the safe and familiar space of their former lives to be in a new space with a former enemy, to create a new space for others to live. Both leaders demonstrated empathy for his new collaborator's opinions, even if they agreed to disagree.

Generosity Is Seen in Cleaving[17]—Being Trusting

Living in South Africa through the early 1990s was like being on a roller coaster at an amusement park, except it was not amusing. The talks often broke down and it seemed like the differences were too great for the leaders to overcome. Shortly after the opening of the Convention for a Democratic South Africa,[18] the differences between these two men became clear for the world to see. De Klerk attacked Mandela for maintaining the military wing of the ANC and not being genuine about finding a peaceful solution. Mandela retorted by calling de Klerk "a product of apartheid."[19] While this outburst revealed the emotional toll that they were paying for being in this new place, it also exposed the lack of trust that existed between them. Overnight, they were able to return to the reason why they embarked on the journey in the first place and the next morning they shook hands and declared their altercation "a closed matter."[20]

16. Mandela, *Long Walk*, 494–96.

17. I will use the three verbs, leave, cleave, and weave that are found in Genesis 2 to describe generosity here. These three verbs are similar in function to beauty, strength, and productivity (*venustas, firmitas, utilitas*), which were immortalized on the medallion that winners of the coveted Pritzker Architecture Prize receive.

18. CODESA began on December 21, 1991, at the World Trade Center in Johannesburg, with more than 220 delegates from nineteen commitment to negotiate: (1) the new constitution, (2) the setting up of the interim government, (3) the future of the homelands, (4) time period for the implementation of the changes, and (5) the electoral system

19. Mandela, *Long Walk*, 519–20.

20. Ibid.

They both knew that they could not achieve the goal of a democratic South Africa on their own. They were in this together, and it was going to require generosity. As we have already seen, the idea of cleaving[21] in the ancient mind was closely associated with: adhere; to glue, to join, but also to follow closely. Before a carpenter can join two pieces of wood, the surfaces will need to be planed and sanded until any they fit perfectly. This is what was going to happen to de Klerk and Mandela over the next few years.

There were many more altercations to come because truth for Mandela and de Klerk were two very different propositions. From my perspective, the darkest moment for these two leaders was possibly in the autumn of 1992, when the negotiations for a new constitution completely stalled. In response to a communication from de Klerk, Mandela concluded his strongly worded response by saying:

> Find a way within yourself to recognise the gravity of the crisis. The starting point for this is that you stop deluding yourself that it is the ANC and its Allies programme of mass action which is the cause of the crisis. It would be a grave mistake if your government thinks that resorting to repression and the use of the military and police power that it commands can be a means of resolving the conflict. Find a way to address the demands we have placed before you with regards to the negotiations deadlock and those relating to the violence so that negotiations can become meaningful and be vested with the urgency that the situation requires. Failure to respond in this way can only exacerbate the crisis. You may succeed in delaying, but never in preventing, the transition of South Africa to a democracy.[22]

Both men were facing severe pressure from within their own ranks at this time. De Klerk had to call for a referendum on the March 17, 1992, to get a mandate from white South Africans, and he succeeded.[23]

Mandela, on the other hand, was at risk of being undermined by more radical factions within the ANC who were very popular with the mass

21. The Hebrew word for cleave is *davag*.

22. Letter from Nelson Mandela to F. W. de Klerk: State President of the Republic of South Africa, July 9, 1992 http://www.anc.org.za/show.php?id=4141, accessed October 12, 2012.

23. He promised to resign as President if he did not receive a mandate for his policies. He received more than 66 percent support from white voters and this stopped the momentum of the opposition in the white parliament. See Ottaway, *Chained Together*, 199.

democratic movement. So-called black on black violence erupted across South Africa as malevolent forces began to control the minds of those who were losing hope. At a rally after yet another massacre, Mandela shouted at the top of his voice to be heard above the crowd: "We must accept that responsibility for ending violence is not just the government's, the police's, the army's. It is also our responsibility . . . We should put our own house in order." This is not what the angry crowd wanted to hear and so they shouted back, but Mandela raised his voice again. This time there was no question about who was the leader, when he said, "I am your leader, I am going to give leadership. Do you want me to remain your leader?" When they answered, "Yes!" Mandela continued, "Well, as long as I am your leader, I will tell you, always, when you are wrong."[24]

These two leaders were being shaped by the forces of history to cleave. While their own personal weaknesses were being revealed and the uneven edges of their ideological differences were being planed away, they could see that trusting each other and being flexible provide the only way through this liminal space between the old and the new South Africa.

In December 1992, in secret bilateral talks between Mandela and de Klerk, a major breakthrough occurred when they both demonstrated their trust and flexibility. The prophetic words of de Klerk's predecessor, P. W. Botha, came true: "We must adapt otherwise we shall die."[25] This was literally the case; the country was erupting in violence and no more political vanity could be tolerated. They found a way that required trust and adaptability: There would be a government of national unity for five years based on proportional representation; thereafter a simple majority rule would govern South Africa.

The public received news of this agreement in the spring of 1993, and on April 27, 1994, the first democratic election was held in South Africa. During one of the televised debates that led to the election of Nelson Mandela as the president and F. W. de Klerk as his deputy, Mandela took de Klerk's hand saying, "In spite of my criticism of Mr de Klerk, Sir, you are one of those I rely on . . . I am proud to hold your hand for us to go forward."[26]

24. Meredith, *Nelson Mandela*, 495.

25. Ibid., 345. P. W. Botha went on to say: "A white monopoly is untenable in Africa of today . . . A meaningful division of power is needed between all races."

26. Mandela, *Long Walk*, 617, and de Klerk, *Last Trek*, 332.

When the glue is applied, the carpenter will trust the joint he has prepared. In the same way a generous mind will seek truth, do the hard work behind the scenes, to have a strong, trustworthy joint that can flex when it is under strain.

Generosity Is Seen Weaving—Being Productive

Despite the stress of their situations and the strains on their relationship, they were willing to be stretched and to extend themselves for the sake of the common goal—a new and better South Africa.[27] Weaving this new social fabric, this new community, would demand generosity and willingness to lay it all down in service the people they loved.

During the Rivonia Sabotage trial, Mandela was one of the ten ANC leaders who faced the death penalty. They were accused of 221 acts of sabotage designed to overthrow the apartheid government. He famously used this opportunity to explain his opposition to apartheid, but it is his love for South Africans that is most striking in his concluding remarks:

> I have cherished the ideal of a democratic and free society in which *all persons live together in harmony and with equal opportunities.* It is an ideal which I hope to live for and to achieve. But if needs be, it is an ideal for which I am prepared to die.[28]

While I was an adjunct faculty member at the University of the Western Cape, a university set up by the Nationalist Government to educate the so-called colored people of South Africa, de Klerk was the minister of education. His conservative political behavior led to many mass actions by faculty and staff in the late 1980s.

I, for one, did not expect that he was going to initiate political reforms in South Africa when he became the president in 1989. The collapse of communism, the international sanctions against South Africa, and his revulsion at the far right might have motivated him to make contact with Mandela a few months after becoming president. But it was his love for the people of South Africa that penetrated the pomp and ceremony of his

27. For Mandela, the goal was a "free society in which all people live in harmony." He was willing to give it all up, even to die, to achieve this goal. See Mandela, *Long Walk*, 322.

28. Ibid., 368. (Italics mine).

presidential inauguration, as he sensed a calling "to save *all* the people of South Africa"[29]

In the face of such love there is no place for the lust of power. It is about being in the service of those you feel called to. De Klerk immediately called for an election after his inauguration. His platform was reform: the normalization of politics in South Africa, which included the removal of racial discrimination for society and the establishment of a new constitution that would be the bedrock of a new South Africa. The support of his government slumped to a mere 41 percent of the white votes during the election, and he could only barely make the case that he had a mandate for change. Like Mandela, he too was willing to risk it all for the sake of a better community.

When the final results came in and it was clear that the ANC would lead the new government of national unity, the generosity of these men was on display again. Even though a case could be made for electoral malpractice, de Klerk refused to challenge the outcome.[30] Mandela, on the other hand, was relieved that the ANC did not achieve 66 percent of the electoral vote—the number they needed to approve the constitution on its own. His explanation reveals his heart:

> I was relieved; had we won two-thirds of the vote and been able to write the constitution unfettered by input from others, people would argue that we had created an ANC constitution not a South African constitution. I wanted a true government of national unity.[31]

The *productivity* of a generous mind is seen in the community that is created through a commitment to service for the sake of a common good. Instead of living lives with a narrow, individualistic mentality, generosity reclaims the ancient wisdom that human life is best lived in community. As such, this generosity evokes within us a desire to be hospitable, a desire to create and serve the community that gave birth to us.

29. Sparks, *Tomorrow*, 100. (Italics mine).

30. de Klerk, *Last Trek*, 336.

31. Mandela, *Long Walk*, 619.

Generosity in Certainty and Doubt

As we have seen, de Klerk and Mandela faced many conflicting thoughts and emotions as they met in secret to negotiate the end of apartheid; that the uncertainties that they were facing militated against generosity. Perhaps like a jury, de Klerk and Mandela had to struggle within the tension between certainty and doubt, and hoped that they could be reasonable when it would be easy to be unreasonable—but fortunately generosity prevailed and they stayed true to their vocations as leaders.

In the lead-up to the election on April 27, 1994, there was a sudden escalation of violence. As South Africans prepared themselves for the elections, stories like these made headlines:

> The KwaZulu/Natal region remained a tinder box over the weekend—despite several high-profile peace initiatives. In one incident, the home of African National Congress regional premier candidate Mr Jacob Zuma was torched by a mob on Saturday night in Nxamalala, near Inkandla, in Northern Natal.[32]

> More than thirty people were killed and hundreds injured in battles in the Johannesburg area yesterday as tens of thousands of Zulus converged on the city centre to demonstrate their support for King Goodwill Zwelithini.[33]

> Pre-election stockpiling of non-perishables has spread countrywide, despite Eskom assurances that there was no chance of a nationwide black-out over the election period . . . In the Western Cape, stores reported that candles, blankets, black plastic bags, canned foods and dry foods such as mealie meal and rice had disappeared from supermarket shelves as quickly as they came in.[34]

> With only nine days to go before South Africa's first all-race elections, there are fears that the security forces may not have the manpower to prevent violence and intimidation seriously affecting voter turnout in some parts of the country.[35]

> Nine people were killed and ninety-two injured in central Johannesburg yesterday in South Africa's largest bomb blast. Police said the 90kg car bomb—almost twice the size of that in the 1983

32. *Sowetan*, March 28, 1994.
33. *Business Day*, March 29, 1994.
34. *The Star*, April 5, 1994.
35. *City Press*, April 17, 1994.

> Pretoria bombing—went off on the corner of Bree and Von Wielligh Streets just before 10am, instantly killing a pavement fruit seller and causing extensive damage to the ANC's regional and national headquarters, as well as surrounding buildings.[36]

> A bomb blast rocked a taxi rank near the Randfontein station early yesterday, just a few hours before an explosive device was thrown at minibus taxis parked under a bridge near Westonaria.[37]

More than eighty bombs exploded across the nation in 1993. Political parties were at each other's throats. Chris Hani, the leader of the South African Communist Party, had been assassinated in his driveway. Day after day, South Africans were anesthetized by the news of another massacre. In the face of doubts, de Klerk and Mandela remained generous in mind and resolute to create a new South Africa that was: beautiful, safe, and benefits everyone.

Doubt could easily have derailed one or both of these men as it derails many who set out to develop a generous mind-set. It is therefore important to understand the place and function of doubt in our thought life.

Beyond Reasonable Doubt

In courts of law, if we can believe the courtroom dramas beamed across the world, the jury's goal is to make a decision beyond a reasonable doubt. Beyond a *reasonable doubt* is a term that refers to certainty that comes from a preponderance of the evidence, a certainty that is not absolute, but one which makes sense in the light of the given evidence. A *reasonable doubt* is not an imaginary or giddy doubt; it cannot be based upon sympathy or prejudice. Rather, it is based on reason and common sense. It is logically derived from the evidence or absence thereof. Alfred Lord Tennyson (1809–1892) once said, "There lives more faith in honest doubt, believe me, than in half the creeds." If there is reasonable doubt, the accused must go free; this is what generosity requires.

So, when the judge is asking for a judgment that is "beyond a reasonable doubt," she is asking for more than reason to be applied; what is being asked for is a generosity of mind. I think that being generous of mind means being loyal to reason in order to make sense of something, but also

36. *Business Day*, April 25, 1994.

37. *The Citizen*, April 26, 1994.

accepting the human limitations on our ability to reason things out—we accept that we are not omniscient as human beings. Human reason is fallible. Therefore, with this new frame of mind comes a humility that is different to the pride[38] that we described earlier. We accept that the conclusions that we have drawn and the theories that we have constructed are our best attempts at understanding, but are not our last attempts. If this generosity were not present, Mandela and de Klerk would not have concluded that they should meet again.

A jury is required to apply common sense to the question of whether a person is guilty of a crime. They must make sense of the evidence in a way that leads them to a conclusion that is beyond a reasonable doubt. In other words, they need to be *reasonably certain* of their decision. Have they resolved the question beyond *a reasonable doubt*, or, we could say, with *reasonable certainty*? I know that as one of many Afrikaner families living through the 1980s in South Africa, we then had *reasonable certainty* that my eighteen-year-old brother, who had become a conscripted soldier in the South African Defence Force, was doing the right thing. While he was away, we needed the certainty that apartheid was worth defending, worth his life. But as a family we also needed to go on with normal life, and it was the other *reasonable certainties* of life—security of income, strength of family relationships, and so on—that made it possible.

If we follow this line of thinking, then we can also see that it would be possible that the jury could be *unreasonably certain* about their decision. In this instance the jury is overly confident in their decision-making abilities. There is a lack of humility and they are confident that they can provide the final word on the subject—they have the power and power is truth.[39] In this scenario generosity is crowded out.

Ferdi Barnard was a hitman for the apartheid government of South Africa. I was in the same school and church youth group as Ferdi and his siblings. Because Ferdi is a few years older than I am, my contact with him was limited, but there are a few strong memories that I still have today. I remember watching Ferdi play rugby. He was an inspiration to all of us as his heroics on the sports field often resulted in success for our rugby teams. He was a strong young man with strong opinions. I remember one day

38. When we discussed *hupsoma* in the previous chapter.

39. Foucault, "Power and Subjection," 230. Foucault explains the relationship between power and truth. He writes, "We are subjected to the production of truth through power and we cannot exercise power except through the production of truth."

at a youth camp when an evangelist attempted to manipulate Ferdi, but he would have nothing to do with it. He did what most of us would have liked to do; he walked out. I do not think that I saw Ferdi at youth group or at church after that incident. After Ferdi graduated from high school he signed up to fulfil his national duty in one of the armed forces of South Africa. His parents would have known that there was a real chance that he might die in his attempt to protect the policies of the South African Government.

There is a good chance that the Barnard family, like so many other Afrikaner families, would have been *certain*, even *unreasonably certain*, that the Nationalist Government's version of reality in South Africa was worth killing for. They would have hoped against hope that their son would not be one of the many who would not make it back from combat with the enemies of the State. Imagine the joy when your son comes home from combat. This happened in our home. It happened in the home of the Barnards—it is the joy of death defied. But what happens to this celebration when a few years later, Nelson Mandela is released and the *Truth and Reconciliation Commission* reveals that other Christians trained your son to torture and to kill? This is what the Barnard family had to face. I remember the day when I read the news headline, "Ferdi Barnard Killed David Webster." Webster was an anti-apartheid campaigner and worked tirelessly to end compulsory military duty.

I often wonder what happens to our *unreasonable certainty* when the basis for our certainty is exposed as fraudulent. Does it become even more entrenched, or do we end up in a dark night of the soul in *unreasonable doubt*? One thing is certain: some form of generosity will be required to be free again.

A fourth option is therefore just as possible: the jury could suffer from self-doubt. They could doubt the evidence for and against the defendant. They could disagree with the arguments presented by the defense and the state. They could question the fairness of the judge. This can be described as *unreasonable doubt* and again generosity is all but absent. I knew that I had witnessed police brutality, and after the incident described in chapter 1 I sometimes questioned what we Afrikaners were fighting for, but these questions were too intrusive and so I suppressed them. It could easily tip me into a dark night of the soul. It did not happen in my teenage years, but Emory University was waiting in my future.

Since I think best in pictures, let me illustrate what I am saying. We have two axes. On the vertical axis we can move from being unreasonable to being reasonable as I described earlier. On the horizontal axis we find ourselves somewhere between doubting and being certain (see diagram below).

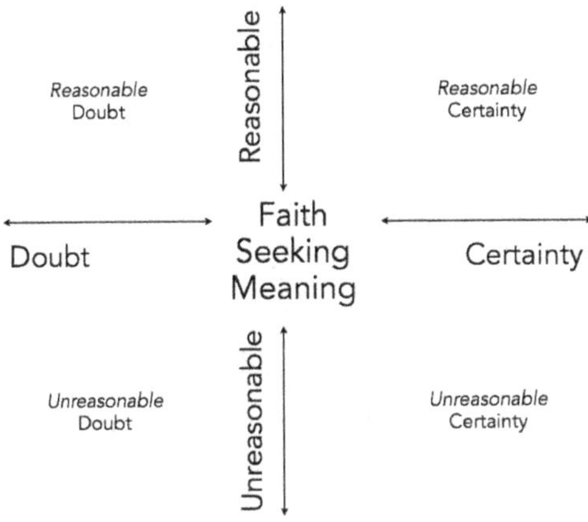

My natural instinct is to suggest that we first progress from *unreasonable certainty* to *unreasonable doubt* as we face times of transition.[40] Then, as we emerge from the dark night of the soul and we begin to experience "new beginnings,"[41] we move on to *reasonable certainty* as a new normal. It would be as if we graduate from one level to move on to the next.

Some developmental theorists[42] would agree that there is some sequence to be observed in the four quadrants. While I think that there may be a case for such a progression, I am concerned that it is too neat a representation of life, and that the messiness of life may defy these tidy categories. Over the months and years that followed Nelson Mandela's release,

40. See Bridges, *Managing Transitions*. He identifies three types of change that can occur in the human life cycle: developmental change, reconstructive change, and change in response to intrusive marker events.

41. Ibid. Bridges identifies three stages in change: endings, neutral zone, and new beginnings.

42. I have already referred to James Fowler's faith development theory. He has identified six different stages or styles of faith—where faith represents our attempt to find meaning. What is significant is that Fowler believes that these stages are hierarchical, meaning that one builds on the other and they are sequential and invariant—it is impossible to skip a stage. I have learned so much from James Fowler, but I no longer hold to the linear model that forms the basis for Fowler's model.

South Africans experienced the roller coaster ride of all four quadrants. In it all, generosity of mind was required, but we will talk more about this later in the book.

Space of Mind

I know that I certainly struggled to remain generous of mind as we lived through the struggle against apartheid on the Cape Flats. To those who know the Cape Flats, this would sound like a contradiction, since the Flats can hardly be a place for generosity. While it is generous as a wide-open, sandy, flat area on the outskirts of Cape Town, it was claustrophobic with a heavy police and military presence. As I already mentioned, it was a war zone, politically, socially, and spiritually. On occasion, some have described the Flats as "apartheid's dumping ground" because it was the home for all those who failed the fingernail and pencil tests of the government. All those people that the apartheid government designated as "non-white," or not "white" enough, were forced out of the more central urban areas because these areas were designated for "whites" only.

Here, I learned that one should also read the second half of Philippians 4:5, "The Lord is near." Perhaps the early church was encouraged to be generous in mind, to have a new mind-set, because the Lord will return soon. They could be generous because their salvation is coming soon. But on the Cape Flats that was not the expectation. Many prayed for the return of Christ, but their prayers were not answered. So this phrase took on a different meaning for me. "The Lord is near," meant that he is present, that I can engage Jesus when I am tormented by my doubts and certainties. And, as I do, I follow Jesus's example of how to live in liminality: I eat the bread that comes from the Father's mouth. It does not matter whether I am in the delights of reasonable certainty or in the despair of unreasonable doubts, Jesus can be engaged; the trajectory of his storyline must be followed.

The Cape Flats became a place of generosity, not just because I made the best friend there, or because I enjoyed some of the best food and hospitality in homes that were being held together by wire and sellotape. It was a generous space where I could explore my doubts and certainties both in times when I was reasonable and when I was unreasonable in my thoughts and actions.

I did not progress neatly from *unreasonable doubt* to *reasonable certainty* because, in my world, doubts and certainties were not mutually exclusive. I did not progress from *unreasonable certainty* to *reasonable doubt* because, in my world, my actions were sometimes reasonable and other times quite unreasonable. It was my experience then, as it is now, that I inhabit all four quadrants of the *reasonable-doubt matrix.* A new, not black and white frame of mind is required to live with doubt and certainty, reason and unreason, as we follow the Story that we find ourselves in.

I sometimes think that these quadrants are like rooms in a house. As we live life, we end up in all of them at some time for some reason. It is not that I am equally at ease in every room, but what I have learned is that they present unique opportunities and challenges. I have favored different rooms at different times of my life, but it is the human ability for faith that enables us to keep the opposing forces in tension with each other. And as we do, a new generous frame of mind emerges.

When I saw Mandela and de Klerk hand in hand as they received the Nobel Peace prize together, I knew that the storyline of Christ demands a new generosity of mind. For some staunch Afrikaners this new way of thinking sprouted its first shoots when they heard him praise de Klerk as "a man of integrity." Or when Archbishop Emeritus Desmond Tutu, on the eve of the tenth anniversary of the Truth and Reconciliation Commission, called for the release of Ferdi Barnard from prison, saying of the very man who was hired to kill him, "Crime does not define the person completely."[43]

A generous frame of mind emerges as we follow the trajectory of the Christ-story through the liminality of the already and the not yet. To develop a theology that employs and generates this kind of generosity is what we need to turn to next.

43. "Forgive Apartheid-Era State Killers—Tutu," *The Independent*, April 8, 2006.

10

Maturing Mind

Toward a Generative Theology

I could not believe what I was seeing. There was a man in my car and he was fast asleep. It was in the early hours of the morning and I had worked till late to finish the last chapter for my doctoral dissertation. The dot-matrix printer made monotonous sounds of passing time as it printed line-for-line, pausing between each line as if to take a breath. I also needed a breath, so I decided that it would save time if I began to pack my car that was parked in the fenced car park of the college. There I found him. I could see that the car window was smashed, the speakers had been ripped from the panel in the back window, and the radio and tape set was on the seat next to where he was sleeping. I tip-toed back to the dormitory to find some help. While someone called the police, another more adventurous student who had seen it all in the townships, stealthily swooped in to awaken the sleepy intruder. Startled by the sudden movement, the dazed burglar dropped the small screwdriver that was still in his hand; he opened his glazed eyes revealing his intoxication, and offered no resistance.

Since I needed to make a deadline for the submission of my dissertation, we had to start the fourteen-hour journey to Pretoria that day. I needed this matter to be resolved, so I returned to the police station as early as I could. The burglar's sister and her husband were already at the police station when I arrived and they were very keen to speak to me. "Please," they pleaded, "Don't lay a charge against him. He is a good boy, but he is with the wrong crowd; this time they will lock him up for sure." They promised to take him away from Cape Town, to a farm where they both worked. Here, they believed he would be able to make a fresh start. I agreed, not because I was generous, my motivation was more utilitarian; the deadline was looming and my car still needed to be repaired. Some years later, my students who knew the legend of the sleepy intruder were delighted to tell me that they heard him speak about the generosity of an Afrikaner who gave him a second chance. I was glad that another James had crossed my path, but it is his family's generative actions that gave him a second chance—they were the *stakeholders and destiny shapers in his life*. They brought him home.

Theology as Home

There is a difference between a house and home. One way this can be explained is by exploring the difference between a brain and a mind. Andrew Newberg and Eugene d'Aquili did some ground-breaking work to help us understand the difference between the two.[1] They tell the story of two Buddhist monks who argued about whether the flag or the wind was moving on their temple. It is reported that the wise patriarch settled the matter by saying it was neither the wind nor the flag that was moving, but that it was their minds that were moving. What these two monks did not know is that we do not really see with our eyes. In reality, our eyes serve only as a lens; ultimately we see with our minds. What they did not understand is that the brain is the structure that manages the process of seeing and the mind has to interpret the information that the brain delivers. In the same way, a house is a structure, but a home is where life is interpreted, where life finds meaning.

Through many complex processes and interrelated structures, information about the flag that the Buddhist monks were looking at is delivered to the vision-point of the cerebrum through the optic nerves of their brains. It is now the work of the mind to answer the questions: What is this? What is going on here? The brain and mind look at the same thing, but the brain has the structural component that performs the physical functions required to make it possible to see, while the mind interprets and seeks to resolve the information that the structures of the brain are processing.

What a brain is to the human mind, a house is to a home. A house, like the brain, consists of building components that provide the structurally

1. Newberg and d'Aquili, "Creative Brain," 53–68.

sound physical environment that is suitable to accommodate human life. The now famous quote of Henry Louis Mencken comes to mind: "A home is not a mere transient shelter; its essence lies in the personalities of the people who live in it."[2] In a home, friends and family, the structure of the space, serves the relationships and the whole becomes greater than the sum of the parts. In homes, adults seek to make a positive contribution to the next generation by providing a generous space. Here, as stakeholders, generative adults invest their time and energy in parenting, mentoring, teaching, caring, and leadership—all to ensure the wellbeing of the next generation.

Many homes have been wrecked on the Cape Flats over the years. The socio-economic furnace created by apartheid required faithful responses from Christians every day. Many Christians on the Cape Flats read their Bibles, attended church and prayer meetings, and this helped them to make sense of the torrid situation they were facing. Pastors, priests, and elders, like parents invested time and energy in nurturing, mentoring, educating, caring, and leadership—all to ensure the wellbeing of the people. But there was not time to dwell on theology too long; there was certainly no room for abstract theology for these believers who lived in shacks, housing projects, or dilapidated houses. The socio-political juggernaut of apartheid was bearing down on them and their theology was often inseparable from action. It was a "theology on the run."[3]

Unfortunately, this was not universal on the Cape Flats. I also noticed that theology was sometimes more like a house than a home. It had all the structures in place, but it did not generate life. Instead of employing and generating generosity in the struggle against the blasphemy of apartheid, some churches retreated into the safe rooms of their church polity and doctrine. Some Bible schools and institutes taught theology as if we

2. The full quotation is, "Such a habitation, it must be plain, cannot be called a home. A home is not a mere transient shelter; its essence lies in its permanence, in its capacity for accretion and solidification, in its quality of representing, in all its details, the personalities of the people who live in it. In the course of years it becomes a sort of museum of those people; they give it its indefinable air, separating it from all other homes, as one human face is separated from all others. It is at once a refuge from the world, a treasure house, a castle, and the shrine of a whole hierarchy of peculiarly private and potent gods." Mencken, "Living in Baltimore," accessed December 11, 2012. http:// www. menckenhouse.org /library/Mencken.HL.1925-02-16.Sun(M).p15c4.On-Living-In-Baltimore.html.

3. Gerkin, *Widening the Horizons*, 60. It is a concept that is similar to Karl Barth's idea of *theologia viatorum*, a theology of pilgrims.

were in a German or American context. Students were "front-loaded" with theory, but the application was left to chance. The hope was that one day they would make the connection when they face real life. When they face real life? Really?

It became obvious to me and the faculty that I was a part of, that this kind of theology was often stingy and sterile. We desired to do theology, not just study it; we longed for a theology that employs and generates generosity.

Towards a Generative Theology[4]

Edward Farley points out that before there were seminaries in the Middle Ages, theology could best be described as *theology habitus*.[5] According to Edward Farley, the church progressively moved away from this approach to theology. During the Middle Ages, theology was the mother of all sciences—theology itself was a "science" (a body of knowledge), and as such, it provided the intellectual context for other scientific inquiry. This all changed with the rational inquiry that accompanied the Enlightenment. According to Farley, *Theology Science* became *Theology Sciences*. During the enlightenment, theology's perceived monopoly on truth was broken; theology was now only one of the many sciences at the universities. The preoccupation was now more with theology's ability to compete with the other sciences that were on offer at the universities. Sadly, in many theological faculties, a break away from communities of faith occurred. Instead of theology being known as an act of practical wisdom about God, it became a "generic term for a cluster of disciplines."[6]

The generative nature of theology is very close to James Fowler's explanation of *theology habitus* as, "theology as knowledge of God pursued through disciplines of prayer, study and liturgical participation, aimed towards the formation of persons and communities in accordance with the

4. In 2001 I pioneered the Openseminary that employs a generative theological methodology. The approach delivers theological training through the six purposeful actions of the Christian life: Theologia, Koinonia, Leitourgia, Kerygma, Diakonia, and Paideia. These purposeful actions become the windows through which biblical, historical, theological, and contemporary issues are examined. Knowledge of practice is thus built up through an integrative inquiry that leads to renewed understanding of the requirements for good practice. This course is offered as Master Degrees in Theological Method in South Africa, Australia, and the USA. See www.openseminary.com.

5. Farley, *Theologia*, 35ff.

6. Ibid., 81.

knowledge of God."[7] This definition assumes, of course, the liminality in which we find ourselves and the need for us to follow Christ along the trajectory of God's story of regeneration. It emphasizes that in the act of doing theology, soul and society are transformed. But what is missing from this definition, and many other definitions, is the reminder that we do theology as generative adults to ensure the wellbeing of the next generation. Yes, we are formed by theology and hopefully our communities are better because of our faith, but let's not forget those who follow will learn from us.

While I am not sure that describing theology as practical goes far enough, Charles Gerkin's description of theology brings us another step closer to generative theology when he points out that "practical theology always takes place in the midst of praxis and is prompted by the situation of 'being in the midst' . . . In that sense practical theology is always, or virtually always, done on the run, so to speak, or in the midst of the necessity of action."[8] Gerkin's emphasis on praxis is especially significant.

Praxis refers to an unusual way of knowing and thinking. Gustav Gutiérrez in his ground-breaking work, *A Theology of Liberation: History Politics and Salvation*, employs *praxis* to refer to purposeful action that is guided by theory.[9] It is not theoretical knowledge that can be acquired through study—though it certainly includes it. Nor is it like the practical know-how of a master chef, although, once again, this kind of knowledge is included. Instead, *praxis* refers to a creative ability to keep theory and practice in tension, although it does more than only keep these in tension; it also integrates them into a pattern in which action and ongoing reflection mutually indwell each other.[10]

This explanation reminds me of our earlier discussion of the divine dance, or the mutual indwelling of the Trinity.[11] Questions that emerge from our contexts and traditional answers are the second couple in the

7. Fowler, *Faith Development*, 13–14. Theology as habitus has received scholarly attention with some disagreeing with the subjective nature of Theology *Habitus*. See Wood, *Vision and Discernment*.

8. Gerkin, *Widening the Horizons*, 60. While I see the need to speak of Practical Theology, it seems to raise more questions than it answers.

9. The Greek word *praxis* has long been used to describe theological activities of oppressed communities. See Gutiérrez, *A Theology of Liberation*, 16–19 and 289–91. Others have applied this concept to the task of theology; see Groome, *Christian Religious Education*; Farley, *Theologia*; and Fowler, *Faith Development*.

10. Fowler, *Faith Development*, 15.

11. Think *perichoresis*.

dance. Like the interplay between theory and practice, the first couple, they take part in the dance called *praxis*. *Praxis* is the mutual indwelling that occurs as theory shapes practice while at the same time, practice is shaped by theory. The same is true when questions demand answers from tradition and tradition helps us formulate questions. Praxis seems to be behind Steve Land's understanding of the task of theology. He writes, "The theological task demands the ongoing integration of beliefs, affections, and actions lest the spirituality and theology fragment into intellectualism, sentimentalism and activism respectively."[12]

Into this creative tension, Jesus, the Word of God, comes, and seemingly loose thoughts, emotions, and actions begin to fit into the structure of life enabled by Christ.[13] Then, the structure of reason, wisdom, and the lawfulness of Christ begins to transform soul and society.[14] But Christ does not come to us as a disembodied truth; he comes as through the authoritative narrative of God's relationship with humankind, and we are invited to join that Story in faith. Our minds and hearts are transformed into theological homes when the Holy Spirit mediates the coming of Jesus, the Word of God, and inhabits our faith-filled attempts to find meaning. The Holy Spirit, as the bond of love, enables Jesus, the Word of God, to inhabit our quest for meaning in everyday life. As we are re-minded by the Story that we find ourselves in, a generous frame of mind is shaped in us—a mind that is able to leave (be present), cleave (be trusting), and weave (be productive) as we become adults in Christ. (See diagram below).

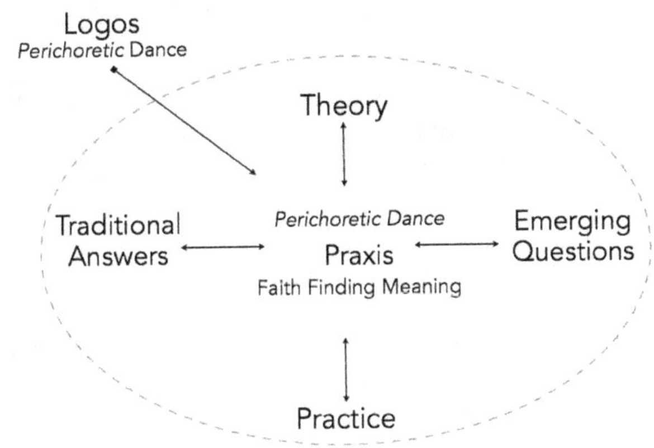

12. Land, *Pentecostal Spirituality*, 41.

13. 2 Cor 10:5 (The Message).

14. Fowler, *Faith Development*, 43.

Generative theology therefore employs and generates generosity as believers pursue the knowledge of God through the integration of: (a) sacred questions that come from our context; (b) the generative tradition of the Story that we inhabit; (c) beliefs that transform us as we follow Jesus through the liminality of the "already and the not yet"; and (d) purposeful actions that create space for life as we attempt to discern the trajectory of God's regenerative action in the world.

In the task of doing theology, generative theology employs and generates generosity in the ongoing integration of questions, traditions, beliefs, and actions in a bid to avoid the entrapment caused by dogmatism, traditionalism, pragmatism, and faddism. While it is beyond the scope of this book to discuss the method and the scope of generative theology, I will give a brief overview here.

Method: Generative Theology Employs Generosity

"It's dog-eat-dog out there! The world doesn't fight fair. We don't live or fight our battles that way. Our weapons are not carnal."[15] But many wars, perhaps the height of carnality, have been fought over method and content of theology. Theologians will not speak to other theologians because they do not have the same view about the rapture, or church leaders will not attend conferences because the speakers are too Catholic, too Charismatic, too Fundamentalist, too Missional, or too Emergent. Christian authors publish books about each other and write web-blog entries that are tantamount to committing character assassination.

Most theological approaches require a deep understanding of the theological tradition that supports the theological reflection. Grenz and Franke once observed that not all beliefs or theological assertions are born equal. They wrote:

> Not all beliefs we hold (or assertions we formulate) are on the same level, but that some beliefs (or assertions) anchor others. Stated on the opposite manner, certain of our beliefs (or assertions) receive their support from other beliefs (or assertions) that are more "basic" or "foundational."[16]

15. 2 Cor 10:3–5 (The Message).

16. Grenz and Franke, *Beyond Foundationalism*.

Conflicts about theology often arise as these foundations are debated. Wentzel van Huyssteen explains why:

> Foundationalism in this epistemological sense therefore always implies the holding of a position of inflexibility and infallibility, because in the process of justifying our knowledge claims, we are able to invoke ultimate foundations on which we construct the evidential support systems of our various convictional beliefs.[17]

The concept of foundations is taken from the world of buildings and construction. Foundations in this world determine the ultimate shape, size, and function of the building, and they must therefore be carefully considered and designed. Because this metaphor is often used in theological education, a lot of time and energy is expended to the basic beliefs and assertions. This foundation determines the theological construction that is true to the brand of Christianity that created it in the first place.

While I believe that foundations are required, it is how they are acquired that concerns me. I wonder who determines what goes into the foundation? Who has the power to make that decision? Who decides what the basic beliefs are? I am sure that by now, as a reader, you will appreciate that my experience of apartheid has made me deeply suspicious of this kind of power and privilege.

I believe that language acquisition is a better metaphor for the role and function of foundations in education. A child does not receive an education in nouns, verbs, grammar, and syntax before she utters her first word. Rather, as she faces the demands of life, competes with siblings for whatever would make her world a better place, she vocalizes her first word. The world stops for a moment, but after a while it gets used to her one-word communication style. Because she is ignored, her words become short phrases, then sentences, and soon paragraphs follow. One could say that her linguistic foundation was being generated, layer for layer, as she used language. Is that not also the way we can acquire the language of theology?

As an artist, I have learned that the first layer of paint on the canvas may or may not be seen when the painting is done. As I paint layer after layer, as I add and scrape paint away, a picture emerges that may be what I had in mind, but often it is not. The canvas under my gaze and the paint on my brush seem to have a life of its own. Just like language, painting is alive and dynamic, and this should also be true for theology.

17. van Huyssteen, *Essays*, 2.

In the spirit of generosity, through leaving, cleaving, and weaving, a foundation for knowing God is being generated. It unfolds like this for me: (1) as I leave the familiarity of traditional questions and answers to be present (leave), to consider the sacred question in the light of the traditional understanding of the Story that I am in; (2) a new answer is concluded when I can trust (cleave) it as I take the next step with Jesus, the Word, through the liminality of the "already and the not yet"; (3) this trustworthy answer will lead me to new productivity (weaving) as I commit myself to purposeful actions that are true to the trajectory of God's regenerative action in the world. (See diagram below).

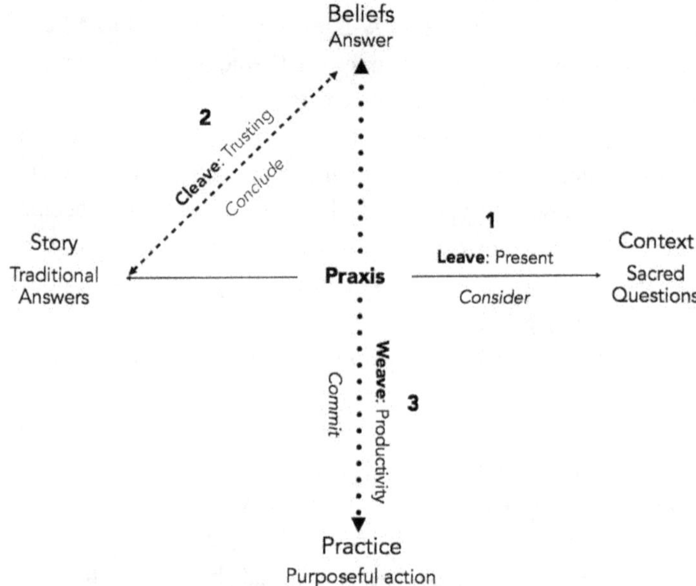

But each answer, I have found, is just the next best answer. Like a layer, it is not the final answer. In time, these productive actions will become practices that will generate new sacred questions (see diagram below). If I do not answer it again, the generation that follows will go through a similar process. My answers cannot be forced on them, but they could help them to be followers of Jesus through finding the liminality of the "already and the not yet." Through this generative cycle, theology finally rids itself of the tyranny of the perfect, final answer.

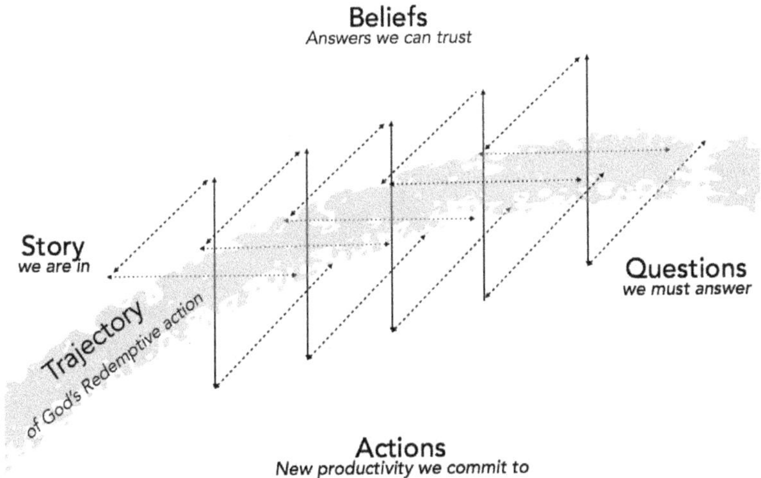

Scope: Generative Theology Generates Generosity

At the most rudimentary level it could be said that theology wants to enable new thoughts and new behaviors in believers. Two well-trodden paths have been followed in theological education or in spiritual formation to achieve this.

The first approach emphasizes knowledge and assumes that if we introduce new ideas and change the thinking patterns of learners, it would lead to a change in their knowledge and behavior. The motto of this approach is: "Think yourself into new beliefs and behaviors." In the Greek world of the Olympic Games, theorists, through detached observation and analysis, advised athletes on how best to prepare for competition. In this tradition, education focuses on knowledge that is born of analytic distance and objectivity.

The second approach places an emphasis on behavior. Proponents of this approach argue that we ultimately arrive at new thoughts and behaviors if we change old behaviors. The motto of this approach is: "Behave yourself into new beliefs and behaviors." Education in ancient Judaism was synonymous with life; it explained life, giving it direction and meaning. The practical nature of this education is seen in a Jewish ancient saying: "Train up a child in the way he should go; and when he is old he will not depart from it."[18] Training was in the ways of life; it was not conceptual thinking that was removed from the practicalities of life.

The danger of an emphasis on thoughts or behaviors is that one may conclude that, once we have acquired the new knowledge or skills, the job is done. While all education involves change, it is also true that not all change is transformation. It is possible to acquire knowledge and skills and remain the same person. From this warning arises the conviction that new knowledge and skills cannot be the ultimate purpose of education, but that the transformation of the learner is a worthier goal.

A transformation of our attitude that dramatically and irreversibly alters the way we are in the world should be the aim of theology. We need to do theology that answers Paul's call:

> Therefore if you have any encouragement from being united with Christ, if any comfort from his love, if any common sharing in the Spirit, if any tenderness and compassion, then make my joy complete by being like-minded, having the same love, being one in spirit and of one mind. Do nothing out of selfish ambition or vain conceit. Rather, in humility value others above yourselves, not looking to your own interests but each of you to the interests of the others.[19]

18. Prov 22: 6.
19. Phil 2:1–4 (NIV).

On the Cape Flats, and perhaps even more now, I longed to do theology that employs and generates generosity. While transformative learning involves experiencing a deep shift in the basic premises of thought and actions, these shifts, we believe, are enabled, mediated, and integrated by a transformation in our inner core, our being. As we mentioned in an earlier chapter, Paul Tillich says that we suffer from the loss of being what we were created to be and of becoming what we were supposed to become.[20] The anxiety that marks human existence is the result of our separation from God. Theology should therefore not contribute to this separation from God and others; it should generate a new space in which we can be with God and others while we live this life here on earth. Theology that is generative will therefore seek to integrate knowing, doing, and being through the generosity that marks God's actions in this world.

The Generosity of Presence

Generosity in mind creates new space when there is no space. In the first act of creation, it seems to me, God made room for all of his creation. There was a "time," as we pointed out earlier, when time and space did not exist as we know it. There was no sun and earth; there was only God—Father,

20. See Tillich, *Courage to Be*, 44–48. Also, Tillich distinguishes three types of anxiety: that of fate and death (ontological), that of emptiness and loss of meaning (spiritual), and that of guilt and condemnation (moral) (ibid., 41).

Son, and Holy Spirit in an eternal co-existence called the Trinity. But there was no space outside of God. This spaciousness was externalized when God decided to make people. He decided to "leave" in order to be present with his creation. He called forth space and placed the universe within. How all of that happened is part of public debate. The mystery of this goes beyond the banal debate of creationism and evolution. Did God say, "Let there be . . . " and as a result the heavens and the earth were shaped in one big cosmic bang? Or did God say, "Let there be . . ." and the heaven and earth were formed in seven literal days? All of that seems unimportant when it is compared to the mystery of God externalizing his spaciousness in order that we can live. What matters is that, in a generous act God made space for life when there was no space outside of him. This generosity should be reflected in the knowing, being, and doing that theology generates.

The Generosity of Trust

In the creation story we are told that God created through his Word. God spoke creation into existence. This Word is more than just God's breath that passes through his vocal chords to make words—it points to something, or rather someone, far more profound. As we have already noted, James Fowler observed that "our effort to elaborate the outline of a theology of God's creative work led us to see that there is purposefulness and intentional structure built into the space, time and matter that came into being in creation."[21] Christ is the Word through whom all creation came about and he is the purpose that is built into the heart of creation.[22]

As we trust the design of God, as we live with Christ as our wisdom and within his righteous processes, we live in freedom. As God's workmanship, we are created in Christ to have freedom—to live in freedom and never to return to a life of slavery and one-up-manship. This evokes in those who want to live in Christ the desire to know this designer and his design more intimately.

The amazing space that God is making for us in Christ requires that we do not stay the same. There are many references in the Christian scriptures that point to the imperative of growth and transformation. Unlike buildings that are destroyed by earthquakes because of their overly rigid

21. Fowler, *Stages of Faith*, 42.

22. Ibid, 43

structures, we are designed for change, designed to morph and change as the Word of God comes to us.

Jacob Firet a Dutch theologian first introduced me to this idea when I was still a doctoral student. According to Firet, God comes to us by his Word in the form of proclamation, teaching, and counselling. When his Word is trusted, a force-field of power is created that enables two things to happen. First, through the arrival of the Word we gain a deeper understanding of life. Secondly, we are enabled to change.[23] It is widely argued in theological circles that there are opportune moments—*Kairos moments*—when God's love breaks into human existence and humans are changed as a result. This evokes in those who are open to the in-breaking power of God, a desire to grow—to be formed by the Word.

The Generosity of Productivity

In the Old Testament God makes a covenant with Abraham that he and his descendants would be both productive as they join God in his work in this world and a conduit of God's blessing to the nations. God says to him:

> I will surely bless you and make your descendants as numerous as the stars in the sky and as the sand on the seashore. Your descendants will take possession of the cities of their enemies, and through your offspring all nations on earth will be blessed, because you have obeyed me.[24]

The productivity of a generous mind is seen in the community that it creates and mutuality that it inspires. When God made space, he enabled human relationship, but more than that, God enables human beings to enter into a mutual relationship with Trinity. Our lives are now hidden in Christ, in God. The blessing that flows in had to flow through them to the nations. In the New Testament this becomes a focus once again. In Ephesians 2:10, Paul suggests that every human being, as masterpiece, has a place, a task that has been prepared for it in advance.

This points us once again to a vocational understanding of life, that as the workmanship of God, we are living our lives in and through a God who is on a mission. This evokes in us a desire to hear God's call to partnership; it challenges us to respond to that call in *service* to him.

23. Firet, *Agogisch Moment*.

24. Gen 22:17–18.

Theology that is generative always takes place in the midst of God's redemptive actions in the world. Theology therefore enables us to discern where we are most needed in the mission of God and where the world most needs God's intervention. The place God calls us is the place where faith seeks meaning and meaning seeks faith. So, when we engage the arts, commerce, and sciences in our context we can expect to encounter the questions that God's activity in this world is stirring up. Generative Theology is therefore always "in process"; it is never finalized.

11

Peace of Mind

God's Smile on My Mind

Today was the beginning of a new era. The polls would open early and I would get the chance to vote for the first time as a thirty-three-year-old person. There was very little doubt in my mind that the ANC would win and that Nelson Mandela would become the first president of the New South Africa.

The polling booth was at the local school, not too far from where we lived in Cape Town. We would walk there, and many others had the same idea. It was an amazing experience; hundreds of people were lining the streets. We very quickly became part of a queue of people of every imaginable color, size, and shape. At first it felt strange since no one really spoke; it was as if we were waiting for something bad to happen. Behind us was a black nanny with white children in a baby-stroller; in front of us was a colored suburban family who had recently moved into the "white" neighborhood. No one spoke; all were trapped in their own thoughts. But as we waited and the queue slowly edged forward, the chatter became more noticeable.

Nature, however, had another plan. The rain clouds pushed over Table Mountain like a big tablecloth and soft rain began to fall on us all. Within seconds, black and white people shared umbrellas, newspapers, and whatever else they could find to hide under.

The result of the election was quickly announced and Nelson Mandela became the first democratically elected President of South Africa, with de

Klerk as his deputy. I was deeply moved on the day of his inauguration when he quoted from Marianne Williamson's book, *A Return to Love*:

> Our deepest fear is not that we are inadequate. Our deepest fear is that we are powerful beyond measure. It is our light, not our darkness that most frightens us. We ask ourselves: "Who am I to be brilliant, gorgeous, talented, and fabulous?" Actually, who are you not to be? You are a child of God. Your playing small does not serve the world. There is nothing enlightened about shrinking so that other people won't feel insecure around you. We are all meant to shine, as children do. We were born to make manifest the glory of God that is within us. It's not just in some of us; it's in everyone.[1]

It was time for apartheid to go and for South Africans to shine, to be generous, to make manifest the glory of God that is in all of us. South Africa, the rainbow nation, was born and I think God smiled.

God Is Happy

I think God smiled on Election Day on the 27th of April, 1994, because God is in his very being satisfied and happy. In *Mere Christianity*, C. S. Lewis picks up on the happiness of God and links this to the dynamic nature of God. He writes, "In Christianity, God is not a static thing—not even a person—but a dynamic, pulsating activity, a life, almost a kind of drama. Almost, if you will not think me irreverent, a kind of dance."[2]

In his first letter to Timothy, Paul writes about the "The gospel of the glory of the blessed God."[3] The word for "blessed"[4] can easily be translated as "blissful" or "happy." Could it be that God is a happy God? That God has a sense of humor and that his main aim in life is not to ensure that humans never commit a sin? As you would have noticed through these pages, for a long time I thought of God as powerful, stern, and judgmental, but I never thought of God as happy.

It seems I suffered for a long time from the same spiritual condition that plagued many other devout believers. Phillip Melanchthon, the theological genius of the Protestant Reformation and good friend of Martin

1. Williamson, *Return To Love*, 190–91.
2. Lewis, *Mere Christianity*, 175.
3. 1 Tim 1:11 (NIV).
4. Greek is *makarios*. See Liddell and Scott, *Greek English Lexicon*, 484.

Luther, was not immune to it either. It is believed that in desperation Luther once said to his friend that he could sin a little bit because God is able and willing to forgive him.

The same problem was also experienced in America during the eighteenth century. It is now a well-documented fact that even a Calvinist like Jonathan Edwards, a preacher during the great awakening, made the joy of God a dominant theme in his preaching. Edwards said,

> Another part of God's fullness [*sic*] which he communicates is his happiness. This happiness consists in enjoying and rejoicing in himself; and so does also the creature's happiness. It is a participation of what is in God; and God and his glory are the objective ground of it. The happiness of the creature consists in rejoicing in God; by which also God is magnified and exalted. Joy, or the exulting of the heart in God's glory, is one thing that belongs to praise.[5]

He was keen to point out that the trinitarian life is a happy life—Father, Son, and Holy Spirit are a happy community who get along well. If this were not true, heaven would be a miserable place. Life with a grumpy God in eternity would certainly not be described as heaven. If it is not true for heaven, then why do we put up with this notion of God while we live here on earth?

In order to understand the meaning of the word "blessed," we need to remind ourselves that while many translations translate the words of Paul to Timothy as "the glorious gospel of a blessed God," it is not completely satisfactory. The problem with this translation is that *glory* is seen as a modifier of gospel. It is more probable that *glory* is the *content* of the good news. There are varying translations of this verse, but I think it is fair to translate this verse as "the gospel of the glory of the blessed God" and to paraphrase it as "the good news of the tangible demonstration of the presence of a happy God."

You may wonder why I chose "tangible demonstration of the presence" as a paraphrase for *glory*. The word "glory," as we have already seen, is a difficult word to grasp. *Glory* in the New Testament is a combination of the twenty Hebrew words for glory, the original Greek meaning of the word.[6] So, instead of its original meaning of belief, opinion, or reputa-

5. Edwards, *Works*, 101.

6. When the Hebrew Scriptures were translated into Greek, *doxa* was used to translate more than twenty Hebrew words with the result that the meaning of these words has been absorbed in our understanding of *doxa*.

tion, it now also speaks of majesty, brightness, beams of light, and much more. This is because one of the main Hebrew words for *glory*[7] that was translated as glory in Greek Old Testament refers to the light that beamed down onto the Ark of the Covenant. *Glory*, as the beam of God's light on the tabernacle was more than a show—it was a tangible demonstration of God's presence in absolute holiness. So, the priest would certainly lose his life if he dared to enter this space unprepared and unclean.

I prefer to translate *blessed* as *happy*. It would be good and proper to translate it as *blessed*, but this word has become too religious in contemporary English. Paul had two words that he could have used to express this thought. The one would refer to a person who is happy or blessed because people are speaking well of him; and the other emphasizes that God is happy in himself and does not rely on the opinion of others or circumstances to be happy. Paul chose the second option. In human terms, God smiles because he is restful and at peace in himself. I think God smiles.

God Smiles When He Calls Us Friends

We were created in the overflow of this trinitarian life, in God's laughter. "You are worthy, our Lord and God, to receive glory and honour and power, for you created all things, and by your *will* they were created and have their being."[8]

There are so many references to God's *will*[9] throughout the Bible. The frequent use of this term had, in the past, reinforced the notion of the imperialistic God in my mind. It is almost as if, were we to ask God, "Why did you create?" He would answer, "Because I could!"

While it is true that God could act in his sovereign power, I believe that this view does not tell the whole story. Why do dictators do what they do so well? Why did the police torture political dissidents without a care for human rights in the police cells in South Africa? Or today, how is it possible that Zimbabwean president, Robert Mugabe, can violate the human dignity of his own people? The answer is, "They can, and therefore they will." Surely God's motives are more nuanced than the monosyllabic lust

7. Hebrew word *kabod.*
8. Rev 4:11 (NIV). Italics added.
9. Greek word *thelema.*

for power displayed by oppressive governments. Surely his actions are more mysterious than the predictability of malevolent dictators.

Jonathan Edwards would agree that there is more to God's creation than a mere imposition of his will on creation. In the mid-eighteenth century, when Edwards was writing a paper on the purpose of creation—a work that was published posthumously[10]—philosophers of his day had made human happiness the ultimate goal for life. They argued for a form of Epicurean hedonism that suggested that life's goal is to minimize pain and maximize pleasure. Edwards did not agree with them and presented an alternative form of hedonism. Many of Edwards's detractors would have considered hedonism as unbiblical because it would be seen as being incompatible with the Christian doctrine of sin and doing the will of God. Yet, this is not how Edwards approaches his critique of his Epicurean counterparts.

According to this great eighteenth-century theologian, preacher, and philosopher, God created the world for his glory. Hedonism needs to be understood from the perspective of God's glory. If glory is, as we have paraphrased it, the tangible demonstration of God's presence, and *blessed* is the happy restful state of God, then God created the world as a tangible demonstration of his happiness. Happiness is, then, not something to be pursued for its own sake, but rather it comes from God and is a part of God's glory. From this, we understand that God did not create because he could or because he had the power (the way of the oppressor). Instead, he created because it externalized his *happiness*.

Creation is God's smile; we are God's smile.

So what does it mean then when we read in Revelation that "by your will they were created and have their being"?[11] Is this not an iron-fisted legislator at work? I think not, and Edwards as well as others are pointing us to a more layered understanding of God's will.[12] The King James Version

10. Edwards, *The End*, paragraph 114, writes: "Their excellence and happiness is nothing but the emanation and expression of God's glory. God, in seeking their glory and happiness, seeks himself, and in seeking himself, i.e., himself diffused . . . he seeks their glory and happiness."

11. Rev 4:11 (NIV).

12. Most modern translators choose to translate *thelema* as "will." This is a good option, but translation is not an exact science. The number one problem that translators face is that most words operate in a field of meaning, so choosing the right word is not simple. That is why meaning is often lost in translation.

translates Revelation 4:11 as, "For thy *pleasure*[13] they are and were created," because *pleasure* and *desire* are two alternative options that could be used when we translate *will* in Greek.

It would be interesting to substitute *will* with *pleasure* or *desire* in its various occurrences in the Bible. For instance, consider this verse: "For whoever does the will of my Father in heaven is my brother and sister and mother."[14] This translation easily conjures up an image of a group of people who joylessly do what they were told to do—a picture of slavish obedience to the instructions of the one who commanded it. The color and tone of this passage changes significantly when we translate *will* as *pleasure*, "For whosoever shall do the pleasure of my Father in heaven, the same is my brother, and sister, and mother."[15]

When we use the word *pleasure*, the meaning shifts from servile obedience to familial loyalty, from judicious obligation to vocational commitment. I love it when Jesus says that his disciples are no longer servants, they are friends. He explains it like this:

> I've told you these things for a purpose: that my joy might be your joy, and your joy wholly mature. This is my command: Love one another the way I love you. This is the very best way to love. Put your life on the line for your friends. You are my friends when you do the things I command you. I'm no longer calling you servants because servants don't understand what their master is thinking and planning. No, I've named you friends because I've let you in on everything I've heard from the Father.[16]

To understand this shift from slave to friend, we need to understand the relationship between Jesus and his Father. In essence, the earthly Jesus adored his Father. Jesus is the content of the Gospel that Paul speaks about. He was the glory, the tangible demonstration of the happiness of God. Through Jesus, God's delight in creation was demonstrated.

This would have been hard for some first-century people to understand. If you were a first-century Docetist, you would believe that Jesus's physical body was an illusion, that Jesus was a pure spirit who only had

13. John Capper, an Australian theologian and colleague, pointed out to me, that "her majesty's pleasure" can refer to someone being in prison. Pleasure in this context then refers to the Queen's "willed desire."

14. Matt 12:50 (NIV).

15. Bible in Basic English.

16. John 15:11–15 (The Message).

the appearance of being in a human body. This idea comes from Plato's philosophy that all things on earth are mere copies of the eternal forms. These forms exist in a reality that cannot be accessed by the body. The body is therefore unable to contain the eternal.

This notion is smashed when Jesus as the eternal Word of God becomes flesh, when God decides to express divinity in humanity. Jesus is not a mirage; he is what you see, a man who is God and God who is a man. When you see him, you see the happiness of God. You see God smiling.

Jesus affirmed this when he answered a question from one of his disciples: "To see me is to see the Father. So how can you ask, 'Where is the Father?' Don't you believe that I am in the Father and the Father is in me?"

And then he added, "The Father who resides in me crafts each word into a divine act."[17] Jesus established a whole new way of being human—an existence that allows Jesus to let us in on everything he has heard from the Father. We are no longer slaves; we are called friends because we are able to live this human life here on earth in union with God.[18]

Now he asks his friends to live in this new reality that he has opened up for them, a reality where his joy with his Father becomes theirs to share. Their participation in this friendship with him and one another would give them joy that is not dependant on the opinions of people or on circumstance. Their joy would be wholly mature and they would know *happiness*, as they themselves become the tangible demonstration of the happiness of God.

This is a true generosity at work. Jesus says that his disciples are his friends because he has let them in on everything that he has heard from the Father. We are at home with the Godhead. This privileged relationship enables us to live human life here on earth; it enables us to live—to be—our theology. I believe this to be the very essence of *theology that is generative.* Its basic assumption is that God's generosity is seen in that he has reached out in friendship to us. Through the mediation of Christ and the empowerment of the Spirit, we are enabled to live generously. In this friendship we become the tangible demonstration of God's happiness here on earth.

This is where the deepest and most profound meaning and happiness are found. I think that John Piper says it well, "The deepest and most

17. Ibid. 14:9–10 (The Message).

18. Richards, *Practical Theology*, 49. He defines Christian spirituality as "Living a human life in this life in union with God."

enduring happiness is found only in God. Not from God, but in God."[19] I think God smiles.

God Smiles When We Reflect His Glory

C. S. Lewis believed that our problem is not that we seek to be happy, but that we are too easily pleased.[20] Even the church, in his estimation, is guilty of this; he pulls no punches as he writes that we are not passionate enough. "We are half-hearted creatures, fooling around with drink and sex and ambition when infinite joy is offered us, like an ignorant child who wants to go on making mud pies in the slum because he cannot imagine what is meant by the offer of a holiday at the sea."[21]

It seems that this problem has been with us for a very long time. Jeremiah, the so-called "prophet of tears," puts it in graphic terms when he records God's lament: "My people have traded my Glory for empty god-dreams and silly god-schemes."[22] The people had traded the tangible demonstration of God's presence for something less substantial. In doing so, Israel lost the ability to be the tangible demonstration of God's happiness among the nations, which would ultimately mean that they would be colonized by the Babylonians, Assyrians, Greeks, and Romans.

Fortunately, the tragedy of Israel's unfolding story did not deter God in his intention to be tangibly present among the nations through a people who know him and whom he knows. God's determination is recorded by one of the prophets who predicted that Israel would be colonized, that they would be exiled from their own land. In Isaiah we read statements like this:

> I know everything they've ever done or thought. I'm going to come and then gather everyone—all nations, all languages. They'll come and see my glory. I'll set up a station at the centre. I'll send the survivors of judgment all over the world: Spain and Africa, Turkey and Greece, and the far-off islands that have never heard of me, who know nothing of what I've done nor who I am. I'll send them out as missionaries to preach my glory among the nations.[23]

19. Piper, *Desiring God*, 19.
20. See Lewis, *Weight of Glory*, 1–2.
21. Ibid.
22. Jer 2:11 (The Message).
23. Isa 66:18–19 (The Message).

What then happened after the ascension of Jesus should not come as a surprise. The followers of Jesus were instructed to go to Jerusalem and to wait there for the Spirit who would empower them to be God's witnesses in Jerusalem, all over Judea and Samaria, even to the ends of the world. God's determination to raise up a people that would be his glory among the nations was noticeable. So, on the day of Pentecost, in a scene that was reminiscent of the consecration of the Temple in the Old Testament, God's glory, his *glory*,[24] came into the building where they were. Only this time the sound of gale force winds was the tangible clue that God was present in that room.

While the thunderous sound filled the room where they were meeting, something profound was happening. It is possible that the disciples could have anticipated that they would be covered by a cloud, like the time when a cloud covered some of the disciples and Jesus on the so-called Mountain of Transfiguration. John gave a good account of this when he wrote, "A light-radiant cloud enveloped them, and sounding from deep in the cloud a voice: 'This is my son, marked by my love, focus of my delight. Listen to him.'"[25]

Even if they could have predicted that there would be a gale force wind, they could not have anticipated that God's breath would transform them into the living stones of a new temple. This temple would attract the nations. This temple would, however, be a nomadic temple, one that would go where God directed it to go. As this started to happen Luke says,

> There were many Jews staying in Jerusalem just then, devout pilgrims from all over the world. When they heard the sound, they came on the run. Then when they heard, one after another, their own mother tongues being spoken, they were thunderstruck.[26]

We read that the sound did not stop with the wind; it turned into human voices, into human languages. "They couldn't for the life of them figure out what was going on, and kept saying, 'Aren't these all Galileans? How come we're hearing them talk in our various mother tongues?'"[27] These ordinary Galileans were transformed into linguistic savants that

24. I Kings 8:11. The Hebrew is *kabod Yahweh*. In Hebrew *Yahweh* is the covenantal, the relational name of God.

25. John 17:5 (The Message).

26. Acts 2:5–11 (The Message).

27. Ibid.

could speak languages[28] that represented the nations from where these pilgrims came. "They were thunderstruck," says Eugene Peterson. While this newly acquired linguistic ability signalled that the Spirit had come, it also signalled that the Spirit chose them to be the tangible demonstration of God's happiness in this world.

At a psychological level, they were also being transformed. Paulo Freire, an educator among the poor in Brazil, gives us the language to describe what happened to these early believers.[29] The poor can often not think for themselves as their thoughts have been colonized by the dominant ideas of those in power. But the poor are "conscientized" when they develop the critical awareness that gives them the vocabulary to express their own thoughts and values, and even the courage to take action against the oppressive elements of their world.

These very ordinary Galileans, some of whom might even have belonged to the most despised in Palestine, experienced a "conscientization" that transformed the way they viewed God, nation, and self. They became "holy things" through whom God's *happiness* would be made known. Instead of having bread and wine with Jesus, they became the bread and wine. His body is broken for their sake and his blood is spilt to give them a new future. Their lives had been given new significance; they found true happiness as they participated through the Spirit in the dance of God to make him known among the nations.[30]

This meant that they could no longer feel the same about non-Jews or continue to stereotype women. It also meant that economic adjustments were inevitable. While their resources were insufficient, they soon discovered that when one partners with God on a mission that cannot be accomplished through human strength, it opens the door for the mighty wind of God to rush in. I think God smiles.

God Smiles When We Are Reconciled

In very dark days, in the Deep South of the United States of America, William James Seymour, a son of black slaves, became passionate about the

28. Greek word is *glossolalia.*

29. See Johns, "Affective-Conscientization," 154.

30. Gerlach and Hine, "Five Factors," 32–33. They argue that a deep sense of God's presence and his empowerment is one factor that could account for the rapid growth of the Pentecostal movement.

gospel and its relevance for his time. He heard of a preacher by the name of Charles Parham who had a Bible school where he was teaching that God would give the end-time church the ability to speak foreign languages. According to Parham, this would enable the church to reach the nations before the return of Christ.

As a Ku Klux Klan sympathizer, Parham would not allow Seymour to study with his white students, but he allowed Seymour to listen to his lectures through an open window. Very soon after his studies, Seymour became a pastor in Los Angeles and there he saw the first person gifted with this missionary language. Word spread and very soon there was talk of a revival, which today is known as the Azusa Street Revival of 1906. It should not surprise us, however, to learn that there was more to this revival than the gift of speaking in tongues. Seymour believed that the linguistic gift existed for the purpose of interracial reconciliation and community. While speaking in tongues was important to him, he was equally amazed at the miracle of interracial reconciliation.[31]

According to Charles Parham, this miracle was a disgrace:

> Men and women, whites and blacks, knelt together or fell across one another; frequently a white woman, perhaps of wealth and culture, could be seen thrown back in the arms of a big "buck nigger,"[32] and held tightly thus as she shivered and shook in freak imitation of Pentecost. Horrible, awful shame![33]

Seymour was undeterred and not intimidated by the aggressive attacks of his white supremacist former teacher. He demonstrated how a mind, once enlarged by the Spirit, could not return to its original size. This is a case study in Spirit-enabled conscientization.

According to Seymour, this Pentecostal experience was simple to understand: it was nothing more than an increase of God's love.[34] He was convinced that love was the benchmark of this revival. If it did not lead to a deeper love for God and others, it ought to be judged as a counterfeit revival.

31. Foster, *Streams of Living Water*, 119.

32. I am embarrassed to include this quote because of the use of this derogatory term for African-American people. It is hard to believe that this was printed in a church publication.

33. Parham, "Free-Love," 4–5.

34. Foster, *Streams of Living Water*, 120.

Perhaps more than anything else, Seymour's own demeanor was testimony to the fact that "the 'color line' was washed away in the blood."[35] He had every reason to hate white Americans for enslaving his own parents, yet he was a holy, godly, prayerful, meek man who tirelessly worked for reconciliation and unity.[36]

I think that Seymour would agree that if the church is called to be the tangible demonstration of God's *happiness*, then the church has to overcome the divisions that are a result of the fall. It will require a miracle of the Spirit to achieve a unity that breaks through class, race, gender, and cultural barriers.

Even though this was a radically different kind of Pentecostalism to what Parham envisaged, its fruits were undeniable for a season. This revival took place decades before the Civil Rights Movement of the 1960s, and one could only speculate how the American society would have been changed if the revival was not "hijacked" by the fears of some leaders. Maybe black and white Americans would have found a way to create a new society that could have provided the moral leadership for nations like South Africa.

The Azusa Street revival had an echo in the early stories of Pentecostalism in South Africa. Tom Hesmelhalch, who was a co-worker of William James Seymour, came to South Africa in 1908. He is quoted by a special journalist of the Rand Daily Mail as saying, "They [Africans] have come to us, and we have received them. They know who has the power of God."[37]

Just in case one might think that this reporter was sympathetic to the reconciliatory momentum of this movement, the journalist expressed his concern that the non-racial stance of Pentecostals would breed revolution. What follows sounds like it could come from the pen of Charles Parham:

> But perhaps the gravest feature of the spread of this faith is its attitude towards the native races. A fortnight ago one of the native propagandists was bearing testimony at the Zion Tabernacle when a young believer not long away from America fell upon the Kaffir's[38] neck and wept for the wrongs under which the natives are, in his opinion, labouring."[39]

35. Ibid., 115.

36. Ibid., 121.

37. *Rand Daily Mail*, July 7, 1909.

38. I am embarrassed to include this quote because of the use of this derogatory term for the first people of South Africa. It is hard to believe that this was printed in a national newspaper.

39. *Rand Daily Mail*, July 7, 1909.

Even though seemingly powerless, the early Pentecostals in South Africa were empowered as they responded to God's generosity. Most of the first-generation Pentecostals were immigrants who came to South Africa during the rush for diamond and gold in the late nineteenth century. Pentecostalism was just as homeless then as those recent immigrants.

It was taking root in a country where Calvinism was seen as the panacea for the social turmoil that marked the South African socio-political landscape. While Kuyperian Calvinism in South Africa summarized its vision in the slogan, "in separation is our strength," Pentecostalism gave a brief and fragile glimpse of a South Africa where the color line would be erased by the blood of Jesus. Again, one can only speculate what South Africa would be like today if the glimpse had become a compelling vision. I think God smiled.

God Smiles When We Love

As I have mentioned before, some of my earliest memories of being alive are of being in a church building. I have clear memories of waking up under a pew during a mid-week prayer meeting to the cacophonous sound of people speaking in tongues, like the early believers in Jerusalem. From a very young age I became aware that the faith tribe that I belonged to associated speaking in tongues with the presence of God. In fact, there was a lot of angst around this matter. If there was a spiritual lull and the prayers of the faithful were not as fervent as our pastor expected them to be, he would warn that this could be a sign that God was withdrawing his glory from our congregation. There was no doubt in my young mind that when someone *spoke in tongues*, God was in the room with us and that person was as holy as the temple was in the days of the Old Testament. It was as if speaking in tongues was the external sign, a tangible way of knowing that God was present.

While this church did not identify itself as part of a sacramental tradition, speaking in tongues, like the early Christian church, functioned as a sacrament in this community. It was something holy that signified that God was present. Jesus was a sacrament, a tangible sign of God's presence in this world, just as the church since Pentecost had become the sacrament of Christ in this world. As for the church of my youth, the church needed to speak in tongues to be the true sacrament of Christ.

It was only much later that I realized that when we seek the gifts of the Spirit, like speaking in tongues, and not the giver of the gifts, calamity waits. This is so tragically illustrated by the well-known story of Frank Chikane. He grew up and was ordained in one of the largest Pentecostal churches in South Africa. As a young minister he became increasingly aware of the injustices of the South African society. In response to his deeply held theological convictions he joined the South African Student Organization in the seventies, and later became its leader. The political credentials of this organization are beyond any doubt since Steve Biko was its inaugural president in the sixties.

It did not take long before Chikane's political activities landed him in hot water with the government as well as with the white leadership of his denomination. They cold-heartedly defrocked him for his ungodly behavior. It would already be sad if the story ended here, but unfortunately it does not finish with an unfair dismissal. Over the years of activism, this diminutive and softly spoken Pentecostal believer was detained and imprisoned on numerous occasions. On one of these occasions, he was interrogated and tortured by another Pentecostal believer. This believer was ordained and ministered in the same denomination that once ordained Chikane.

I found this story deeply troubling since it points us to more substantial questions about the work of the Spirit. Did the same Spirit who empowered the victim to endure suffering also empower the torturer to victimize? Is it possible for both to claim empowerment from the same Spirit? Would the Holy Spirit empower one to enforce injustice and oppression, and empower another to endure the same? Today, I do not believe that at all.

I find some comfort in the story that Luke tells about the empowerment of the disciples on the day of Pentecost. There is little doubt in my mind that speaking in tongues was an important part of the first-century church and functioned as "a linguistic symbol of the sacred,"[40] but there is clearly more. For the early church, this newly acquired linguistic gift and the other gifts pointed to something even more radical; the way God transforms ordinary people to be the *tangible demonstration of God's happiness—his pleasure* among the nations. Later, as we read the Epistles of Paul, we see that he would not allow the pursuit of the gifts of the spirit for the sake of a religious thrill. There is more to them.

40. Macchia, "Sighs," 47–73. He gives an excellent overview of the different interpretations of glossolalia and offers significant insight of his own. He quotes William Samarin, *Tongues*, as a prime exponent of those who understand tongues as a "linguistic symbol of the sacred."

Paul got hot under the collar when he heard that there were people who thought they could operate in the so-called charismatic gifts with no evidence of the bond of love in their lives. There should be no doubt what he means when he says, "If I speak with human eloquence and angelic ecstasy but don't love, I'm nothing but the creaking of a rusty gate."[41]

Now, I appreciate that love is the trademark of the giver of these gifts and that the gifts of the Spirit are, on their own, not a sure sign of God's presence. When we seek the gifts and not the Giver, calamity of Chikane-like proportions awaits us. That is why Paul places his teaching about love in the heart of his exposition of the gifts.

In the church of my childhood I heard many sermons on the importance of love, but the love being taught was nothing more than an emotional connection with those who were, like us, white and Pentecostal. Since then, I have learned from the Cappadocian Fathers that Paul's reference to love points us to the love within the Godhead. The Spirit is the one who is the bond that personifies the love between the Father and the Son. It is this same bond of love which now draws us into the dance that marks God's existence. It is this that enables Christian community and that makes it possible for slave, master, gentile, Jew, female, and male to be baptized into one new humanity in Christ.[42] I think God smiles.

Feeling at Home with a Happy God

One of the joys of being a lecturer in theology is that I can set tasks for my students that give me a rare glimpse of the life of the church in the amazing city that I live in. In one of the subjects I teach, I ask the students to attend a worship service at a Christian church of a different tradition than their own. Through their reflections, I am taken on an amazing journey of discovery—a journey that reveals the multi-layered and varied nature of the church.

I have been surprised to read that a student could sit through an entire worship service, never once hearing any reference to Scripture while, in another church, any reading that was not taken from the King James Version was disregarded and perhaps even seen as a sign of succumbing to the evil influences of this secular postmodern culture. Speaking of which, some

41. 1 Cor 13:1 (The Message).

42. See 1 Cor 12:13, Eph 2, and Gals 3:28.

churches seem to be quite happy to embrace the trendy communication styles of postmodernity—using visual images and non-directive, dialogical forms of preaching—while others do not seem to think that this is preaching at all.

In some churches, the offering and tithe played a significant role in the worship of God. One student was even asked by someone sitting close to him, "So, how much did you give?" I hoped this was a joke but sadly, apparently not. In contrast, other churches seem to have an allergic reaction to the issue of money, leaving it up to those who support the ministry to make an internet contribution.

Tears of frustration welled up in another student's eyes as he was about to walk out of a meeting where he could not engage God in worship; everything seemed so foreign. The liturgy was mechanical; attention was given to every letter and title of church tradition, but it lacked soul. The faces of those in the cold building were equally stark and lifeless; no one dared to show any sign of joy.

But great was the enthusiasm of those who gathered in another ancient church building. The worshippers were standing close to the priest, dressed in black, as he read the Scripture to them in a hushed tone while tourists surveyed the icons that decorated their building.

Some worship God under laser beams with smoke machines, while others are blessed by the gentle puffs of smoke that are generated by the swinging thurible in the priest's hands. Choirs, musicians, and high-tech equipment are used to create the space for worshippers to encounter God; there is energy and vibrancy with charismatic worship leaders and imported speakers. Others seem to be quite content to light a candle, walk meditatively to the center of an ancient labyrinth in search of Christ, or sip coffee while engaging others in a discussion about the relevance of the Gospel.

While some have family services and discipleship classes, others change their language as they incarnate into the subcultures of our city. One student found it challenging and inspiring to hear gothic Christians have sacred gatherings and refer to confession as "the suicide of the self." Blogs and bulletins, audiovisual announcements created by visual arts departments, professionally produced radio advertisements and photocopied handouts are all used to announce what the church will be doing the following Sunday. "Come and see," some are saying, while others demand that members "go and be."

Renovated factories, cafés, bars, and homes are the meeting places for some believers, while others meet in beautiful cathedrals and modern architectural feats. Some church buildings in the inner city become galleries, and for others, galleries are becoming churches.

One student, who reluctantly committed herself to this assignment, attended a cathedral. It was a really stretching experience, since cathedrals represented dead religion to her. Throughout the meeting her deepest fears were being outwardly confirmed, until the rays of the sun beamed through one of the colored window panes. Suddenly, everything was bathed in rose pink. "See my child," she sensed God say to her, "in my mind you are all the same."

Conclusion

Being the Smile on God's Face

It has been a long journey from the front lawn of my family home in the late 1970s. It has been a journey away from an image of God is an unpleasant, bloodthirsty, despot over nations, whose actions seemed capricious and whose attitudes towards sin, petty. His outburst of anger reminded me of the malevolent schoolyard bully that I often faced.

It was a journey away from a worldview shaped by apartheid and the lucidity of this covenantal interpretation of my Afrikaner history to which I gladly succumbed as a child and a young adult. It was a journey that tells the tale of how I had to be out of my mind in order to discover a new way of being.

As my mind changed about God, I have discovered that God is a happy God who makes space for life. God's story is one of regeneration. Those who join God in his story are infused with his passion to create space, to destroy fatedness, and to liberate those who are entrapped. The Spirit enables ordinary people to live in the liminality of the "already and the not yet." Jesus's life in liminality not only demonstrated how a human life can be in union with God, but also enables human life to become generative.

As my mind changed about God, I have discovered God's generosity as he invites us to enter the dance of the Trinity. Through the dance, God generates a generosity of mind within us—his mind as seen in Christ. Consequently, we begin to shape our lives to respond to what God is doing in this world. It is often not the product of a rational system that provides clear answers to complicated questions. Rather, it is when we are at our wits' end, when we have no more answers, that we do that theology that is most generative. In fact, there may be times that God's generosity is more certain than reason. Paul understands this way of doing theology: "Now I take limitations in stride, and with good cheer, these limitations that cut me down to size—abuse, accidents, opposition, bad breaks. I just let Christ take over. And so the weaker I get, the stronger I become."[1]

As my mind changed about God, I have discovered that those who in an attempt to respond to the call of God to generosity, find themselves in over their heads and live lives that are generative. They find themselves in relationships, contexts, and situations that require empowerment that only God can give. The early Christians experienced this, Desmond Tutu, F. W. de Klerk, and Nelson Mandela, and so do we.

As my mind changed about God, I have discovered that theology, the study of God, needs to employ and generate the generosity. I have called this generative theology in the previous chapter. Those who are out facing the challenges and dangers of everyday life, like my friends on the Cape Flats, know generative theology intuitively. It is a theology that leads to purposeful action. It is a theology that was demonstrated by the early Christian church.

After the resurrection, we meet the disciples behind closed doors. They were afraid of what the Jews might do to them, but then Jesus appeared to them. In a moment of deep care and concern he breathed on them, and they drew great strength from the experience. After the Ascension and before Pentecost, these disciples began to take tentative steps toward the mission that they were called to fulfil.

We find them worshipping in the temple, no longer behind closed doors. They were now even finding a replacement for Judas. It is not that they knew exactly what to do, or even how they should do it, but doing theology on the run was typical for them.

Even when the mission is not as clear as in the case of the disciples in Jerusalem, theology that is generative understands that each generation must seek to define God's mission for its own time and place. It revisits the sacred stories of its tradition in order to engage emerging questions with vigor. Even as faddism looms as an ever-present danger, even while the slippery slope of relativized truth is ready to take them down, they are willing to wade through these obvious dangers in an attempt to be free from the narrow-mindedness that comes with dogmatism, pragmatism, and traditionalism.

1. 2 Cor 12:10 (The Message).

As my mind changed about God, I have discovered that theology is done in community. Theological activity in this environment is not focused on doctrines and the *esoterica* of the Christian faith. It is not primarily interested in speculating about the strength of God or the volume of the body of angels or about the kind of questions that one could contemplate while alone on a deserted island.

A theology that is generative understands that truth is located in God who is community; it understands that we are because we are part of the body of Christ—*ubuntu*. We therefore ask each other how we can together determine where we are most needed in the mission of God and where the world most needs God's intervention.[2] *Then it is the work of a theology that employs and generates generosity* to shape the community to be able to respond faithfully to what God is doing. I think that the theological task is guided by questions such as these:

- As we dance with God, are we creating space for life?
- As we dance with God, are we seeking to be coherent in our faith?
- As we dance with God, do we faithfully live and proclaim the good news?
- As we dance with God, are we adaptable enough to live with certainty and uncertainty?
- As we dance with God, are we an earthly representation of a heavenly *ubuntu*?
- As we dance with God, are we seeking to serve before we are served?

As my mind changed about God, I have discovered that the church, as a community, is essentially a sign and instrument in the world. It represents God's desire to provide a tangible demonstration of his *happiness*. As such, the church might be powerless and marginalized, but when we do theology in everyday life and work, we demonstrate that we *are* the body of Christ in the sense that Christ is present in us and that we are present in the world through the empowerment of the Spirit of Christ.

This means that the church as a sacrament is both a *sign* and an *instrument*, a conduit of "the good news of the tangible demonstration of the presence of a happy God."

2. See Samuel and Sugden, "God's Intention," 146.

As my mind changed about God, I have discovered that my words and phrases, my seemingly clever theological models and systems, can only be a faint echo of God's dynamic presence in this world. When I become unreasonable in my certainty that I am right and that everyone else must therefore be wrong, I am demonstrating the same ignorance as the painter who thinks that she can capture a sunset in shades of green.

As my mind changed about God, I have discovered that theology is a verb and not a noun; that it is done in humility and not from a position of power and self-reliance. When I arrived at theological destinations that seemed like safe harbors of truth, even in the case of this book, it inevitably turns out to be just a resting place along the way.

Bibliography

Adams, Sheena, et al. "Forgive Apartheid-Era State Killers—Tutu," *The Independent*, April 8, 2006.

African National Congress. "Letter from Nelson Mandela to F. W. de Klerk: State President of the Republic of South Africa." Accessed October 12, 2012, http://www.anc.org.za/show.php?id=4141.

Alexander, Lloyd. *The Book of Three*. New York: Macmillan, 2006.

Altizer, Thomas J. J., and W. Hamilton. *Radical Theology and the Death of God*. Indianapolis: Bobbs-Merrill, 1966.

Barth, Karl. *Church Dogmatics*. Translated by Geoffrey William Bromiley and Thomas F. Torrance. Edinburgh: T. & T. Clark, 1975.

Baudrillard, Jean. *Simulacra and Simulation*. Translated by Sheila Faria Glaser. Ann Arbor: University of Michigan Press, 1994.

———. *Simulations*. New York: Semiotext[e], 1983.

Bax, Douglas. "The Bible and Apartheid." In *Apartheid Is a Heresy*, edited by John W. de Gruchy, 114–18. Grand Rapids: Eerdmans, 1981.

Bilezikian, Gilbert G. *Community 101: Reclaiming the Local Church as Community of Oneness*. Grand Rapids: Zondervan, 1997.

Boesak, Allan. "He Made Us All, But. . . ." In *Apartheid Is a Heresy*, edited by John W. de Gruchy, 4. Grand Rapids: Eerdmans, 1981.

Bosch, David. "The Afrikaner and South Africa." *Theology Today* 43, no. 2 (1986) 203–16.

———. *Transforming Mission: Paradigm Shifts in the Theology of Mission*. Maryknoll, NY: Orbis, 1991.

Bouma-Prediger, Stephen. *The Greening of Theology: The Ecological Models of Rosemary Radford Ruether, Joseph Sittler and Jürgen Moltmann*. Atlanta: Scholars Press, 1995.

Bridges, William. *Managing Transitions: Making the Most of Change*. Don Mills, ON: Addison-Wesley, 1991.

Brueggemann, Walter. *Praying the Psalms*. Winona, MN: St Mary's Press, 1986.

Buechner, Frederick. *Wishful Thinking: A Theological ABC*. New York: Harper & Row, 1973.

Canadian Association of Spiritual Care. "Virtual Learning Seminar." accessed February 14, 2013. http://www.spiritualcare.ca/resources/virtual_learning.html.

Chesterton, G. K. *The Victorian Age in Literature*. London: Williams and Norgate, 1914.

Cohen, Allan R., et al. *Effective Behavior in Organizations*. Homewood, IL: Irwin, 1984.

Crites, Stephen. "The Narrative Quality of Experience." *Journal of the American Academy of Religion* 39 (1971) 291.

Dark, David. *The Sacredness of Questioning Everything*. Grand Rapids: Zondervan, 2009.

De Klerk, Frederik W. *The Last Trek—A New Beginning: The Autobiography*. London: Pan Macmillan, 2000.

De Kock, Wynand J. "The Church as a Redeemed, Un-Redeemed, and Redeeming Community." In *Toward a Pentecostal Ecclesiology: The Church and the Fivefold Gospel*, edited by John C. Thomas, 47–68. Cleveland, TN: CPT Press, 2010.

Dykstra, C., and S. Parks. *Faith Development and Fowler*. Birmingham: Religious Education Press, 1986.

Eco, Umberto. *Travels in Hyperreality*. Orlando: Harcourt Brace, 1986.

Edwards, Jonathan. *The Works of Jonathan Edwards*. Peabody: Hendrickson, 2004.

Erickson, Millard J. *God in Three Persons: A Contemporary Interpretation of the Trinity*. Grand Rapids: Baker, 1995.

Farley, Edward. *Theologia: The Fragmentation and Unity of Theological Education*. Minneapolis: Augsburg Fortress, 1983.

Firet, Jacob. *Het Agogisch Moment in het Pastoraal Optreden*. Kampen: Kok, 1982.

Foster, Richard J. *Streams of Living Water: Celebrating the Great Traditions of Christian Faith*. New York: Harper Collins, 1998.

Foucault, Michel. *Critical Theory/Intellectual History*. Cambridge, MA: MIT Press, 1994.

———. "Disciplinary Power and Subjection." In *Power/Knowledge: Selected Interviews and Other Writings 1972–77*, edited by Colin Gordon, 230. New York: Pantheon, 1980.

Fowler, James W. *Faith Development and Pastoral Care*. Philadelphia: Fortress, 1987.

———. *Stages of Faith: The Psychology of Human Development and the Quest for Meaning*. San Francisco: Harper & Row, 1981.

———. "Towards a Developmental Perspective on Faith." *Religious Education* 69, no. 2 (1974) 211.

———. *Trajectories in Faith: Five Life Stories*. Nashville: Abingdon, 1980.

Frost, Michael, and Alan Hirsch. *The Shaping of Things to Come: Innovation and Mission for the 21st-Century Church*. Peabody: Hendrickson, 2003.

Gerkin, Charles V. *The Living Human Document: Re-Visioning Counseling in a Hermeneutical Mode*. Nashville: Abingdon, 1984.

———. *Widening the Horizons: Pastoral Responses to a Fragmented Society*. Philadelphia: Westminister, 1986.

Gerlach, Luther P., and Virginia H. Hine. "Five Factors Crucial to the Growth and Spread of Modern Movements." *Journal for the Scientific Study of Religion* 7 (1968) 32–33.

Gibson, James L., et al. *Organizations: Behavior, Structure, Processes*. Plano, TX: Business Publications, 1985.

Glad, Betty. "Passing the Baton: Transformational Political Leadership from Gorbachev to Yeltsin; from de Klerk to Mandela." *Political Psychology* 17 (Spring 1996) 1–28.

Greene, Robert. *The 48 Laws of Power: Concise Edition*. London: Profile Books, 2002.

Grenz, Stanley J., and J. R. Franke. *Beyond Foundationalism: Shaping Theology in a Postmodern Context*. Louisville: Westminster, 2001.

———., et al. *Pocket Dictionary of Theological Terms*. Downers Grove, IL: InterVarsity, 1999.

———. *A Theology for the Community of God*. Nashville: Broadman & Holdman, 1994.

Groome, Thomas H. *Christian Religious Education: A Shared Praxis Approach*. New York: Harper & Row, 1980.

Guder, Darrell L., and Lois Barrett. *Missional Church: A Vision for the Sending of the Church in North America*. Grand Rapids: Eerdmans, 1998.

Gutiérrez, Gustavo. *A Theology of Liberation: History Politics and Salvation*. Translated by Caridad Inda and John Eagleson. Maryknoll, NY: Orbis, 1973.

Hexham, Irving. "Just Like Another Israel," *Religion* 7, no. 1 (1977) 5.

Hooker, Morna. "The Letter to the Philippians, Vol. XI." In *The New Interpreter's Bible*, 540. Nashville: Abingdon, 2000.

Hooke, S. H. *The Bible in Basic English*. Cambridge: Cambridge University Press, 1982.

Jacobi. *The Way of Individuation: The Indispensable Key to Understanding Jungian Psychology*. Translated by R. F. C. Hall. New York: Harcourt, 1965.

Johns, Cheryl. "Affective-Conscientization: Pentecostal Re-Interpretation of Paulo Freire." DEd diss., Southern Baptist Theological Seminary, 1987.

Kallaway, Peter. *The History of Education under Apartheid, 1948–1994: the Doors of Learning and Culture Shall Be Opened*. New York: Peter Lang, 2002.

La Shure, C. "What is Liminality?" Accessed June 11, 2012, http://www.liminality.org/about/whatisliminality.

Land, Steve J. *Pentecostal Spirituality: A Passion for the Kingdom*. Sheffield: Sheffield Academic Press, 1997.

Lasor, William S., et al. *Old Testament Survey*. Grand Rapids: Eerdmans, 1996.

Lewis, C. S. *Mere Christianity*. New York: Simon & Schuster, 1996.

———. *The Weight of Glory and Other Addresses*. Grand Rapids: Eerdmans, 1965.

Liddell, Henry George, and Robert Scott. *An Intermediate Greek-English Lexicon*. Oxford: Clarendon, 1889.

Macchia, Frank D. "Sighs Too Deep for Words: Towards a Theology of Glossolalia." *Journal of Pentecostal Theology* 1 (1992) 47–73.

Mandela, Nelson. *Long Walk to Freedom*. Boston, Little, Brown and Co., 1994.

McAdams, D. P. "Explorations in Generativity." Presented at a symposium on "Erik H. Erikson: His Life and Legacy," Harvard University Medical School, Cambridge, MA, 1994.

McLaren, Brian. "Doubt: The Tides of Faith." Accessed February 17, 2010. http://www.brianmclaren.net/ emc/archives/ resources/ doubt-the-tides-of-faith-written.html.

———. *A New Kind of Christianity: Ten Questions That Are Transforming the Faith*. San Francisco: HarperOne, 2011.

Mencken, H. L. "On Living in Baltimore." Accessed December 11, 2012. http://www.menckenhouse.org /library/Mencken.HL.1925-02-16.Sun(M).p15c4.

Meredith, Martin. *Nelson Mandela: A Biography*. New York: St Martin's Griffin, 1997.

Moltmann, Jürgen. *The Crucified God: The Cross of Christ as the Foundation and Criticism of Christian Theology*. Translated by R. A. Wilson and John Bowden. London: SCM Press, 1974.

———. *The Trinity and the Kingdom of God*. London: SCM, 1981.

Nauright, John. *Sport, Cultures, and Identities in South Africa*. London: Continuum International, 1997.

Newberg, Andrew, and Eugene G. d'Aquili. "The Creative Brain / The Creative Mind." *Zygon* 35, no. 1 (March 2000) 53–68.

Nouwen, Henri. *The Return of the Prodigal Son*. New York: Image, 1994.

Ottaway, David. *Chained Together*. New York: New York Times Press, 1993.

Parham, Charles F. "Free-Love." *The Apostolic Faith* 1, no. 10 (December 1912) 4–5.

Parker, Palmer J. *A Hidden Wholeness: The Journey toward an Undivided Life*. San Francisco: Jossey-Bass, 2004.

Parks, Michael. "'Racial Purists' May Have Black Ancestors, Author Says: S. Africa Book Stirs Whites' Anger." *Los Angeles Times*, March 5, 1985. http://articles.latimes.com/1985-03-05/news/mn-12467_1_controversial-book.

Patterson, Sheila. *The Last Trek: A Study of the Boer and the Afrikaner Nation*. London: SCM Press, 1964.

Peck, M. Scott. *The Road Less Traveled: A New Psychology of Love, Traditional Values, and Spiritual Growth*. New Jersey: Simon & Schuster, 1978.

Pelikan, Jaroslav J. *The Christian Tradition: A History of the Development of Doctrine*. Chicago: University of Chicago Press, 1971.

Pentecostal Theological Seminary. "Full Catalog." Accessed February 13, 2013. http://www.ptseminary.edu/cat/fullcatalog.pdf.

Peters, Ted. *Sin: Radical Evil in Soul and Society*. Grand Rapid: Eerdmans, 1994.

Pienaar, S. W. *Glo in U Volk: D.F. Malan as Redenaar, 1908–1954*. Cape Town: Tafelberg, 1964.

Pinnock, Clark. *Flame of Love*. Downer's Grove: IVP, 1996.

Piper, John. *Desiring God: Meditations of a Christian Hedonist*. Portland: Multnomah, 1986.

Rad, Gerhard Von. *Old Testament Theology*. New York: Harper, 1962.

Reid, W. Stanford. "Preaching Is Social Action." *Christianity Today* 15 (June 1971) 10.

Richards, Lawrence O. *A Practical Theology of Spirituality*. Grand Rapids: Academie/Zondervan, 1987.

Rienecker, Fritz, and Cleon Rogers. *Linguistic Key to the New Testament*. Translated by Cleon Rogers. Grand Rapids: Regency Reference Library, 1980.

Rushdie, Salmon. *Shame*. New York: Aventura/Vintage, 1984.

Samarin, William. *Tongues of Men and Angels*. New York: Macmillan, 1972.

Samuel, Vinay, and Chris Sugden. "God's Intention for the World." In *The Church in Response to Human Need*, 146. Grand Rapids: Eerdmans, 1987.

Sanders, Edith R. "The Hamitic Hypothesis; Its Origin and Functions in Time Perspective." *The Journal of African History* 4, no.4 (1969) 521–32.

Schultz, Hermann. *Old Testament Theology—The Religion of Revelation in Its Pre-Christian Stage of Development*. London: T. & T. Clark, 1898.

Seow, C. L. "Face." In *Dictionary of Deities and Demons in the Bible*. 2nd ed., edited by Karel van der Toorn, et al., 323. Leiden: Brill, 1999.

Shillito, Edward. "Jesus of the Scars." *Areopagus Proclamation* 10 (2000).

Silva, Moises. *Philippians*. Grand Rapids: Baker Academic, 2005.

Sparks, A. *Tomorrow is Another Country: The Inside Story of South Africa's Road to Change*. New York: Hill and Wang, 1995.

Spencer, Aida B. *Beyond the Curse: Women Called to Ministry*. Nashville, TN: Thomas Nelson, 1985.

Stevens, R. P. *The Other Six Days*. Grand Rapids, MI: Eerdmans, 1999.

Tillich, Paul. *The Courage to Be*. Fontana Library, 1952.

———. *The Shaking of the Foundations*. London: S.C.M. Press, 1949.

Torrance, James B. *Worship, Community and the Triune God of Grace*. IVP Academic, 1996.

Torrance, Thomas F. *The Christian Doctrine of God: One Being Three Persons*. Edinburgh: T. & T. Clark, 1996.

Tutu, Desmond. *No Future without Forgiveness*. London: Rider, 1999.

United Nations. "International Convention on the Suppression and Punishment of the Crime of Apartheid." Accessed February 10, 2012. http://untreaty.un.org/cod/avl/ha/cspca/cspca.html.

Vaillant, G E., and E. Milofsky. "The Natural History of Male Psychological Health: IX. Empirical Evidence for Erikson's Model of the Life Cycle." *American Journal of Psychiatry* 137 (1980) 1348–59, quoted in D. P. McAdams, "The Redemptive Self: Generativity and the Stories Americans Live By." *Research in Human Development* 5, no. 2–3 (2006) 81–100.

Van Huyssteen, Wentzel. *Essays in Postfoundationalist Theology*. Grand Rapids: Eerdmans, 1997.

Verkuyl, Johannes. "The Dutch Reformed Church in South Africa and the Ideology and Practice of Apartheid." *Reformed World* 31 (June 1971) 204.

Vicedom, Georg F. *The Mission of God: An Introduction to a Theology of Mission*. Translated by Gilbert A.Thiele and Dennis Hilgendorf. Ft Wayne, IN: Concordia, 1987.

Volf, Miroslav. *After Our Likeness: The Church as the Image of the Trinity*. Grand Rapids: Eerdmans, 1998.

Westerhoff, John H. "A Journey Together in Faith." In *Bringing up Children in the Christian Faith*. Minneapolis: Winston, 1980.

Willard, Dallas. *Renovation of the Heart: Putting on the Character of Christ*. Colorado Springs: NavPress, 2002.

Williamson, Marianne. *A Return to Love: Reflections on the Principles of a Course in Miracles*. New York: Harper Collins, 1992.

Wilt, J., et al. "Exploring the Relationships between Eriksonian Developmental Scripts and Interpersonal Adjustment." *Journal of Adult Development* 17 (2010) 156–61.

Wood, Charles. *Vision and Discernment*. Atlanta: Scholars, 1985.

Wright, N. T. *Jesus and the Victory of God*. Minneapolis: Fortress, 1996.

———. *Luke for Everyone*. London: SPCK, 2001.

www.ingramcontent.com/pod-product-compliance
Lightning Source LLC
Chambersburg PA
CBHW060339100426
42812CB00003B/1059

* 9 7 8 1 4 9 8 2 6 8 2 6 4 *